# The MBLEx Content Unlocked

## The Key to Passing the MBLEx

By Charles Everett

# Table of Contents

# Preface

The idea to create this study guide came about through conversations I had with my fellow massage therapy students concerning the MBLEx standardized licensing exam. The California Massage Therapy Council's (CAMTC) requirement to pass the MBLEx (Massage and Bodywork Licensing Examination) or the BCETMB as of January 1, 2015 produced an array of comments, many of which were worrisome in regards to being confident of passing the exam. I then discussed the idea with my instructor who encouraged me to produce the work.

After researching the Federation of State Massage Therapy Boards (FSMTB) website to find study material and finding none at that time, I then researched what study material was available on the internet. I found several sources that had positive feedback, but I also noticed that approximately 25% of the feedback was negative or stated the material did not help. I decided that the best way to pass the MBLEx was to create a study guide based on the content outline found on the FSMTB.org website.

The FSMTB candidate handbook lists 12 reference texts that were frequently used as resources. This study guide is based on 6 of those reference texts, several referenced organization websites mentioned in these texts, my massage therapy classroom objectives and notes, as well as my knowledge and 12 years of experience as a NSCA-CPT (National Strength and Conditioning Association Certified Personal Trainer). The information presented in the study guide follows the format of the FSMTB Content Outline, is easy to read, and comprehend. I believe it covers 75%-85% of what you need to know.

I suggest that in addition to this study guide you use any and all reference material that would assist you in passing the MBLEx. I recommend viewing the DVD associated with Trail Guide to the Body, your own personal notes and classroom material, the 20 case studies found in Mosby's Fundamentals of Therapeutic Massage that cover at least 80% of the common conditions seen by massage professionals, the free MBLEx questions found on the internet to test your knowledge, and the glossary of terms found in the back of your textbooks.

I welcome your feedback and wish you success with your test.

Charles Everett

# Anatomy & Physiology 12%

## System Structure and Function

### The Chemical Level

**Atoms** are the smallest particle of an element that retains and exhibits the properties of that element; made up of smaller particles called protons, neutrons, and electrons.

**Molecules** are a combination of two or more atoms.

**Elements** are substances composed of a single kind of atom.

### Three types of Chemical Bonds

**Ionic bond**: bond in which one or more electrons from one atom are removed and attached to another atom, resulting in positive and negative ions which attract each other.

**Covalent bond**: bond in which one or more pairs of electrons are shared by two atoms.

**Polar covalent bond**: bond that is electrically neutral because they have the same number of protons and electrons.

### Basic chemical reactions and the concept of pH

**Metabolism**: is the process taking place in living organisms whereby the cells are nourished and carry out their activities.

**Anabolism**: is the process of building up of larger molecules from smaller ones.

**Catabolism**: is the breaking down of larger substances into smaller ones.

**pH**: is actually a measure of hydrogen concentration in body fluid; the pH of the body is 7.4, which is slightly **alkaline**; pH lower than 7 has more hydrogen ions and is **acidic;** pH higher than 7 has fewer hydrogen ions and is **alkaline**.

**Inorganic compounds**: are chemical structures that do not have carbon and hydrogen atoms.

**Organic compounds**: are chemical compounds that have carbon and hydrogen atoms (carbohydrates, proteins, lipids, and nucleic acids: **DNA & RNA**).

**Enzymes**: are proteins that act as catalysts for chemical reactions in metabolism while remaining unchanged themselves; are involved in the process of releasing energy from nutrients (carbohydrates, fats, and proteins).

**DNA (deoxyribonucleic acid)**: genetic material of the cell that carries the chemical "blueprint" of the body.

**RNA (ribonucleic acid)**: a type of nucleic acid consisting of a chain of nucleotides that contain the sugar ribose and the nitrogen bases adenine, guanine, cytosine, and uracil.

## The Cellular Level (Components and Function)

**Cell** is the basic unit of all living matter; all animals and plants are composed of cells.

**Cytoplasm**: is all of the substance within the cell wall other than the nucleus.

**Nucleus**: the main central body of living cells that contains the genetic information for continuing life.

**Cell membrane**: permits soluble substances to enter and leave the protoplasm.

**Endoplasmic reticulum**: two varieties; **smooth endoplasmic reticulum** involved in the metabolism of fats and **rough endoplasmic reticulum** found in cells in which large amounts of protein are made.

**Golgi apparatus**: collects the products of cell synthesis, synthesizes carbohydrates, and holds protein molecules for secretion.

**Lysosomes**: digests proteins, carbohydrates, and other foreign substances that enter the cell.

**Mitochondria**: contains enzymes for releasing energy and converting it to useful forms for cell operation in the form of **adenosine triphosphate (ATP)**.

**Ribosomes**: sites where amino acids are combined to create various proteins.

## Phases of Cell Division

**Interphase**: stage in the life of a cell during which chromosomes are uncoiled and all normal cellular functions except mitosis are underway.

**Prophase**: occurs when chromosomes, composed of DNA, become larger and more defined; can be seen within the cell duplicated as two coiled strands called chromatids.

**Metaphase**: chromosomes arrange themselves around the center of the cell in a plane called the equatorial plane and are held in place by microtubules.

**Anaphase**: the duplicated chromatids are separated and pulled toward the centrioles by shortening microtubules.

**Telophase**: the stage when the chromosomes reach the centrioles (small bodies) and begin to uncoil.

## The Tissue Level (Four Tissue Types)

**Epithelial Tissue**: is a thin protective layer or covering that functions in the process of absorption, excretion, secretion, and protection; they line cavities, form glands, and specialize in moving substances into and out of the blood.

Epithelial tissues are classified by shape: **squamous** (flat), **cuboidal** (small cube shape), and **columnar** (tall or rectangular).

Epithelial tissues make up **three types of membranes**: a membrane is a thin, sheetlike layer of tissue that covers a cell, an organ, or structure.

*Cutaneous membranes* cover the surface of the body (skin, 16% of body weight).

*Serous membranes* line body cavities not open to the external environment and cover many of the organs.

*Mucous membranes* are found on the surface of tubes that open directly to the exterior (respiratory, digestive, reproductive, and urinary tracts).

**Connective Tissue**: binds structures together, provides support and protection, and serves as a framework.

Connective tissue can be categorized as: loose connective tissue, dense connective tissue, and specialized connective tissue.

**Loose Connective Tissue**: *Areolar* – binds the skin to the underlying tissues and fills the spaces between the muscles (known as superficial fascia); *Adipose* – has an abundance of fat-containing cells; acts as a protection against heat loss and stores energy in the form of fat molecules; found between the muscles, around the surface of the heart, around the kidneys, abdominal membranes, and just beneath the skin; *Reticular* – provides framework of the liver and other lymphoid organs.

**Dense Connective Tissue**: *Regular* – tendons (attach muscle to bone), ligaments (attach bone to bone), aponeurosis (wide flat tendons); *Irregular* – muscle sheaths and joint capsules.

**Cartilage**: *Fibrocartilage* – found between the vertebrae and in the pubic symphysis, where strong support and minimal range of movement are required; *Hyaline* – cartilage consisting of fine white fibers; found in the nose, trachea, and on the end of bones and in movable joints; *Elastic* – the most resilient of cartilages and is found in the external ear, larynx, and similar structures.

**Specialized Connective Tissue**: *Bone* – connective tissue in which the intercellular substance is rendered hard by mineral salts, chiefly **calcium phosphate** and **calcium carbonate**; the skeletal structure; *Liquid* - is represented by blood, lymph, and interstitial fluid.

**Muscle Tissue**: the main characteristic of muscle tissue is its ability to provide movement by shortening through contraction; three types of muscle tissue – **skeletal muscle tissue**, **smooth muscle tissue**, and **cardiac muscle tissue**.

**Nerve Tissue**: found in the brain, spinal cord, and associated nerves; nerves act as channels for the transmission of messages to and from the brain and various parts of the body; divided into two types: **neurons**, the actual functional units, and **neuroglia**, which connect and support neurons.

# Circulation

All parts of the body are linked to the Cardiovascular System. The **Cardiovascular System** can be compared to the cooling system of a car. The basic components include a circulating fluid (**blood**), a pump (**the heart**), and an assortment of conducting pipes (a network of blood vessels: **arteries**, **capillaries**, and **veins**).

## Formation of Blood Cells

Red blood cells (**erythrocytes**) are formed in the red bone marrow; White blood cells (**leukocytes**) are produced in the spleen, lymph nodes, and red bone marrow.

**Blood** is a specialized fluid connective tissue that (1) distributes nutrients, oxygen, and hormones to each of the 75 trillion cells in the human body; (2) carries metabolic wastes to the kidneys for excretion; and (3) transports specialized cells that defend peripheral tissues from infection and disease.

**Blood** consists of: (1) **Plasma**, the liquid matrix of blood; (2) **Red blood cells (RBCs)** or erythrocytes transport oxygen and carbon dioxide; (3) White blood cells (**WBCs**) or leukocytes are components of the immune system; (4) **Platelets** or **thrombocytes** aid in blood clotting.

On average there are **5-6 liters of blood** in the cardiovascular system of an adult man, and **4-5 liters** in an adult woman.

**Plasma** makes up approximately 55% of the volume of blood. It functions to regulate fluid balance and pH and to transport nutrients and gases. It is derived from the food and water taken into the body. There are three major classes of plasma proteins:

**Albumins** (about 60%) are important in the transport of fatty acids, steroid hormones, and other substances.

**Globulins** (approximately 35%) include **immunoglobulins**, also called **antibodies**, attack foreign proteins and pathogens; and transport globulins bind small ions, hormones, or compounds.

**Fibrinogen** (about 4%) is the largest of the plasma proteins and is essential for normal blood clotting.

Albumins and Globulins can attach to **lipids** (fats) such as triglycerides, fatty acids, or cholesterol that is not water soluble. **Lipoproteins** readily dissolve in plasma and this is how insoluble lipids are delivered to peripheral tissues. The liver is the primary source of plasma proteins.

**Red blood cells (RBCs)** account for slightly less than half of the total blood volume. RBCs or erythrocytes transport both oxygen and carbon dioxide within the blood stream.

**Hemoglobin** is a RBC protein responsible for the cell's ability to transport oxygen and carbon dioxide. Hemoglobin gives blood its characteristic red color. **Oxygenated** hemoglobin has a bright red color, whereas **deoxygenated** hemoglobin has a deep red color.

The **ABO system** is the best known grouping method for blood type. It has four blood types/groups, **A,B, AB**, and **O**. **Blood type O** is the universal donor and **blood type AB** is the universal recipient.

**Leukocytes (WBCs)** are scattered throughout peripheral tissues. WBCs help defend the body against invasion by pathogens and remove toxins, wastes, and abnormal or damaged cells. There are **two major classes** of leukocytes: (1) **granular leukocytes** or **granulocytes** and (2) **agranular leukocytes** or **agranulocytes**.

<u>**Granular leukocytes**</u> are subdivided into neutrophils, eosinophils, and basophils.

*Neutrophils* are usually the first WBCs to arrive at an injury site; they specialize in attacking and digesting bacteria.

*Eosinophils* are phagocytic cells, which are attracted to foreign compounds that have reacted with circulating antibodies.

*Basophils* migrate to damaged tissues and release histamines, aiding the inflammation response.

<u>**Agranular leukocytes**</u> are subdivided into monocytes and lymphocytes.

*Monocytes*, the largest WBC, usually arrive at the injury site shortly after the first neutrophils and are highly mobile phagocytic cells.

*Lymphocytes* are the primary cells of the **lymphoid system** and are responsible for specific immunity. They include: **T cells** (which enter peripheral tissues and attack foreign cells directly); **B cells** (which secrete antibodies that attack foreign cells or proteins in distant portions of the body; **NK cells** (which destroy abnormal tissue cells; they are important in preventing cancer).

**Platelets** are flattened, membrane-enclosed packets derived from **megakaryocytes** (enormous cells with large nuclei). Platelets transport chemicals important to the clotting process, form a temporary patch in the walls of damaged blood vessels, and after a clot has formed, actively contract reducing the size of the clot and pulls together the cut edges of the vessel wall.

## The Heart

A small organ roughly the size of your clenched fist, located in the **mediastinum**, the space between the lungs. The heart's four muscular chambers: the **right atrium** and **ventricle**, and the **left atrium** and **ventricle** work together to pump blood through a network of blood vessels between the heart and the peripheral tissues.

This network is subdivided into two circuits: the **pulmonary circuit** carries carbon dioxide- rich blood from the heart to the gas exchange surfaces of the lungs and returns oxygen-rich blood to the heart. The **systemic circuit** transports oxygen-rich blood from the heart to the rest of the body's cells, returning carbon dioxide-rich blood back to the heart.

The **right atrium** receives carbon dioxide-rich blood from the systemic circuit and the **right ventricle** discharges this blood into the pulmonary circuit. The **left atrium** collects oxygen-rich blood from the pulmonary circuit and the **left ventricle** ejects this blood into the systemic circuit.

The heart is located in the **pericardial cavity** situated between the pleural cavities in the mediastinum. The heart is lined by the **pericardium** (a serous membrane) and contains a small amount of lubricating fluid, called the **pericardial fluid**.

### **The heart wall contains three layers**:

The *Epicardium* is the visceral pericardium; it covers the heart's outer surface.

The *Myocardium* is the muscular wall of the heart.

The *Endocardium* is the epithelium covering the inner surfaces of the heart.

The **Tricuspid Valve**, located between the right atrium and right ventricle, allows blood to flow from the right atrium into the right ventricle through two great veins, the **superior vena cava** and **inferior vena cava** and through the **coronary sinus** (via the veins of the heart/coronary veins).

The **Pulmonary Semilunar Valve**, positioned between the right ventricle and pulmonary artery, directs deoxygenated blood from the right ventricle into the pulmonary arteries (pulmonary circuit) as blood travels to the lungs.

The **Bicuspid** or **Mitral Valve**, located between the left atrium and ventricle, allows oxygenated blood to flow only from the left atrium into the left ventricle.

The **Aortic Semilunar Valve**, situated in the orifice of the aorta, permits oxygenated blood to be pumped from the left ventricle into the aorta (systemic circuit).

The **Cardiac Cycle** consists of periods of atrial and ventricular **systole** (contraction) and atrial and ventricular **diastole** (relaxation/filling).

Cardiac muscle tissue contracts on its own; this is called **automaticity** or **autorhythmicity**.

The **pacemaker cells** found in the **sinoatrial (SA)** node (**cardiac pacemaker**) normally establish the rate of contraction. **Blood pressure** is the amount of pressure exerted by the blood on the walls of the blood vessels. It is measured with a **sphygmomanometer**. An average, healthy young adult has a blood pressure of 120/80. Blood pressure is highest during contraction of the heart (**systole**), the top number and is lowest when the heart is relaxed (**diastole**), the bottom number.

**Bradycardia** is a heart rate that is slower than normal; **Tachycardia** is a heart rate faster than normal.

**Shock** is a condition that results when the blood supply to vital organs becomes inadequate, causing diminished function of these organs. **Four types of shock**: *cardiogenic shock* results from defective heart function (heart does not pump enough blood); *septic shock* is caused by a bacterial infection; *hypovolemic shock* results from a loss of blood or other bodily fluids; and *anaphylactic shock* results from an allergy or overreaction of the immune system.

## The Blood Vessels

**The Arteries** are thick-walled muscular and elastic vessels that transport oxygenated blood from the heart.

*Elastic arteries* or conducting arteries transport large volumes of blood away from the heart. Examples of elastic arteries include the pulmonary and aortic trunks and their major branches (pulmonary, common carotid, subclavian, and common iliac arteries).

*Muscular arteries* or distribution arteries transport blood to the body's skeletal muscle and internal organs. Examples of muscular arteries include the external carotid artery of the neck, the brachial arteries of the arms, the femoral arteries of the thighs, and the mesenteric arteries of the abdomen.

**Arterioles** control the blood flow between arteries and capillaries.

By constricting (**vasoconstriction**) or relaxing (**vasodilation**) the arterial walls, the sympathetic division of the ANS can regulate and control the blood flow to each organ.

**Capillaries** are the smallest blood vessels and connect arterioles with venules. The most important function of the capillaries is the two-way transport of substances between the flowing blood and the tissue fluids surrounding the cells.

Substances move through the capillary walls by the process of diffusion, filtration, or osmosis.

**Venules** are the microscopic vessels that continue from the capillaries and merge to form veins.

**Veins** are thinner-walled blood vessels that carry deoxygenated and waste-laden blood from the capillaries back to the heart. Veins have valves to prevent blood from flowing backward and act as a venous pump to move blood toward the heart.

### Hepatic Portal Circulation

The purpose of **hepatic portal circulation** (via the **hepatic portal vein**) is to deliver blood from some parts of the gastrointestinal tract to the liver. Blood is drained from the digestive organs, spleen, gall bladder, and pancreas and is delivered to the liver. The hepatic portal vein transports absorbed nutrients, white blood cells from the spleen, poisonous substances that were absorbed in the nutrients and waste products.

### Movement of Substances Into and Out of Cells

**Passive Transport** is the transportation of substance across the cell membrane without the use of energy.

**Diffusion** is a process in which substances move from an area of higher concentration to an area of lower concentration.

**Filtration** is a process in which blood pressure pushes fluids and substances through the capillary wall and into the tissue spaces.

**Osmosis** is a process in which substances move from an area of lower concentration to an area of higher concentration, resulting in the equalizing of the concentrations.

**Active Transport** is the transport of substances into or out of a cell using energy (**ATP**).

# Digestive

The **Digestive System** is composed of the **alimentary canal** and the **accessory digestive organs**. The **alimentary canal** (**gastrointestinal** or **digestive tract**) is a muscular tube that extends from the lips to the anus (about 30 feet). It consists of the:

**Mouth** or **oral cavity** - food is **masticated** (chewed) by the teeth and mixed by the tongue with secretions (**amylase**) from the salivary glands (**saliva** contains enzymes that begin to digest carbohydrates). This action prepares the food into a soft ball called a **bolus** that slides down the throat and is swallowed by voluntary and reflex actions of the muscles of the pharynx.

The **Pharynx** (throat) - is a five inch muscular passageway that houses the digestive and respiratory tracts.

**Esophagus** – the bolus is propelled and churned by a rhythmic wave-like motion (**peristalsis**) throughout the entire length to the opening of the **cardiac sphincter**.

**Stomach** – food passes through the cardiac sphincter and enters the stomach, where it is churned with gastric juices secreted from glands in the wall of the stomach that contain **hydrochloric acid** and protein digesting enzymes.

**Small Intestine** – the longest part of the alimentary canal consists of three parts: the **duodenum** (most of digestion takes place), **jejunum** (most of the absorption takes place), and **ileum** (absorption of food into the blood and lymph is the major function); intestinal juices, secretions of **bile** from the liver (emulsifies fat, stored in the **gall bladder** & carried through the common bile duct) and pancreatic fluids (digests proteins, carbohydrates, and fats) from the pancreas are poured into the duodenum.

**Large Intestine/Colon** – waste materials move through the **iliocecal valve** into a small pouchlike part of the large intestine called the **cecum**; functions of the colon include storing, forming, and excreting waste products of digestion and regulating the body's water balance; bacterial action synthesizes some B-complex vitamins and vitamin K; the colon begins on the right side of the body with the **ascending colon**, travels across the abdominal cavity and forms the **transverse colon**, continues down the left side to become the **descending colon**, forms an S-shape known as the **sigmoid colon** and empties into the **rectum** (temporary storage area for waste).

**Accessory Digestive Organs**: teeth, tongue, salivary glands, pancreas, liver, and gall bladder.

*Salivary glands*: (3) located in the mouth, release salivary amylase (**ptyalin**) to begin the digestion of sugars.

*Pancreas*: located behind the stomach, produces enzymes (amylase, trypsin, and lipase) that is excreted into the small intestine through the pancreatic duct**; islets of Langerhans** produce the hormones insulin and glucagon; insulin regulates the movement of glucose.

### Six Basic Processes of the Digestive System

**Ingestion** – Food enters the mouth.

**Propulsion** – Food must be propelled from one organ to the next.

**Mechanical Digestion** – Mixing of food in the mouth by the tongue, mastication (chewing) with the teeth, churning of food in the stomach and segmentation in the small intestine.

**Chemical Digestion** – Food molecules are broken down into their building blocks by enzymes.

**Absorption** – transport of digested end products from the lumen of the **GI tract** to the blood or lymph is absorption.

**Elimination** – removal and release by defecation of solid waste products (feces) from food that cannot be digested or absorbed.

### The Peritoneum and Its Associated Structures

The **peritoneum** is the mucous membrane that lines the abdominal cavity to prevent friction of the major organs.

**Parietal peritoneum** is the portion lying against the body wall.

**Visceral peritoneum** is the portion surrounding each organ.

**Peritoneal cavity** is defined as the fluid-filled space between the parietal and visceral peritoneum.

# Endocrine

Ductless glands depend on the blood and lymph to carry their secretions to various affected tissues; the *main function* of the **endocrine system** is to assist the nervous system in regulating body processes.

**Hormones**, chemical substances manufactured by the endocrine glands, are specialized so that they act on specific tissues (target organs) or influence certain processes in the body.

<u>**Pituitary gland**</u> (**Master gland**) located in a depression on the sphenoid bone called the stella turcica; the hormones it secretes stimulate or regulate other endocrine glands; regulated by impulses and secretions from the hypothalamus.

*Anterior pituitary* (hormones & function):

**ACTH** (adrenocorticotropin) stimulates adrenal cortex to produce cortical hormones; aids in protecting body in stress situations.

**TSH** (thyroid-stimulating hormone) stimulates the thyroid to produce thyroxin.

**FSH** (follicle-stimulating hormone) stimulates growth and hormone activity of ovarian follicles; stimulates growth of testes; promotes development of sperm.

**HGH** (human growth hormone) promotes growth of all body tissues.

**LH** (Luteinizing hormone) causes development of corpus luteum at site of ruptured ovarian follicle in women; stimulates secretion of testosterone in men.

**Lactogenic hormone** (prolactin) stimulates secretion of milk by mammary glands.

*Posterior pituitary* (hormones & function):

**ADH** (antidiuretic hormone; vasopressin) promotes reabsorption of water in kidney tubules; stimulates smooth muscle tissue of blood vessels.

**Oxytocin** causes contraction of muscle of pregnant uterus; causes ejection of milk from mammary glands.

<u>**Pineal gland**</u> (third eye/crown chakra) is a tiny gland in the brain within the diencephalon and surrounded by pia mater (hormones & function):

**Melatonin** seems to be related to regulation of the 24-hour circadian rhythm.

**Thymus gland** is located deep to the sternum and mediastinum of the thorax and between the lungs at the level of the fourth and fifth thoracic vertebrae (hormones & function):

**Thymosin** is important in the development of T-lymphocytes.

**Adrenal glands** are situated on top of each kidney.

*Adrenal cortex* (hormones & function):

**Cortisol** (95% of glucocorticoids) aids in metabolism of carbohydrates, proteins, and fats; active during stress.

**Aldosterone** (95% of mineralocorticoids) aids in regulating electrolytes.

**Sex hormones** can influence secondary sexual characteristics in male subjects.

*Adrenal medulla* (hormones & function):

**Epinephrine** and **norepinephrine** increase blood pressure and heart rate; activate cells influenced by the sympathetic nervous system plus many not affected by sympathetic.

**Pancreas** located behind the stomach has both endocrine and exocrine functions.

*Pancreatic islets* (hormones & function):

**Insulin** aids transport of glucose into cells; required for cellular metabolism of foods, especially glucose; decreases blood sugar levels.

**Glucagon** stimulates the liver to release glucose, thereby increasing blood sugar levels.

**Parathyroid glands** are situated on each lobe and behind the thyroid (hormones & function):

**Parathormone** regulates the exchange of calcium between the blood and bones; increases calcium level in blood.

**Thyroid gland** is situated on either side of the trachea (hormones & function):

**Thyroid hormones** (**thyroxine** and **triiodothyronine T3**) increase metabolic rate, influencing both physical and mental activities; required for normal growth.

**Calcitonin** decreases calcium level in blood.

**Ovaries** are a pair of glandular organs located within the pelvic area.

*Ovarian follicle* (hormones & function):

**Estrogens** (estradiol, estriol, and estrone) stimulate growth of primary sexual organs (uterus, tubes) and development of secondary sexual organs such as breasts; involved in various aspects of menstrual cycle.

<u>**Corpus luteum**</u> is located in the ovaries (hormones & function):

**Progesterone** stimulates development of secretory parts of mammary glands; prepares uterine lining for implantation of fertilized ovum; aids in maintaining pregnancy.

<u>**Testes**</u> are located in the male scrotum (hormones & function):

**Testosterone** stimulates growth and development of sexual organs (testes, penis, others) plus development of secondary sexual characteristics such as hair growth on the body and face and deepening of voice; stimulates maturation of sperm cells.

<u>**Placenta**</u> located in female womb when pregnant (hormones & function):

**Chorionic gonadotropin** stimulates the ovaries to release progesterone during early pregnancy.

**Estrogen** and **progesterone** helps to keep the uterus receptive to the fetus and placenta during pregnancy.

## How the Body Responds to Stress

**Stress** is associated with the adrenal glands and their secretion of the "**flight**-or-**flight**" hormones. The principal adrenal hormones are **adrenaline** and **cortisol**; they give us a physical and mental boost that heighten our senses, sharpens our reflexes, and prepares our muscles for maximum exertion.

In conjunction with the **pituitary** and **hypothalamus**, adrenaline and cortisol affect most of the internal systems (muscle tone increases, blood pressure rises, and breathing deepens). Blood is directed toward the skeletal muscles and nervous system; digestion virtually stops.

# Integumentary

**Integument** means covering or skin; the skin is the largest organ of the body

## Functions of the Skin

**Protection**: the skin protects the body from injury and bacterial invasion.

**Heat regulation**: healthy body temperature is approximately 98.6 degrees F; as changes occur, the blood and sweat glands of the skin make the necessary adjustments in their functions.

**Secretion** and **excretion**: sweat (**sudoriferous**) glands excrete (eliminate) perspiration; oil (**sebaceous**) glands secrete (produce & release) **sebum**, which is a lubricant.

**Sensation**: the papillary layer of the dermis provides the body with a sense of touch; nerves supplying the skin register sensations such as heat, cold, pressure, and touch; nerve endings are most abundant in the fingertips.

**Absorption**: the skin has limited powers of absorption through its pores.

**Respiration**: the skin breathes through its pores; oxygen is taken in, carbon dioxide is discharged.

## The Layers of the Skin

The **epidermis** is the outermost layer of the body and forms a protective layer covering every part of the body.

The *Stratum corneum* is the outermost layer; the protoplasm of the cells changes into a protein called keratin, forming a waterproof covering.

The *Stratum lucidum* is the next nearly invisible layer of clear cells.

The *Stratum granulosum* (granular layer of the skin) consists of cells that look like granules.

The *Stratum spinosum* varies in thickness and consists of irregularly shaped cells containing melanin (coloring matter) of the skin; helps protect the sensitive cells from strong solar rays.

The *Stratum germinativum* is the deepest layer of the epidermis; a single layer of cells well nourished by the dermis; they are the only skin cells that undergo **mitosis**.

**Dermis** is the inner layer of our skin and is much thicker than the epidermis; composed of dense connective tissue (collagen and elastin fibers), provide much of the structure and strength of our skin; hair, sebaceous and sweat glands, and nails originate in the dermis.

***Papillary layer*** (directly beneath the epidermis) contains the papillae, the conelike projections made of fine strands of elastic tissue that extend upward into the epidermis.

***Reticular layer*** contains fat cells, blood and lymph vessels, sweat and oil glands, hair follicles, and nerve endings.

***Subcutaneous tissue*** is regarded as a continuation of the dermis; fatty tissue gives smoothness and contour to the body, provides a reservoir for fuel and energy, and serves as a protective cushion for the upper skin layers.

## Accessory Structures of the Skin

**Hair** protects the skin and orifices of the body, keeps us warm, and assists in our sense of touch; hair is composed of dead cells that have become **keratinized** (hardened); tiny muscles, called **arrector pili**, attach to hair follicles and cause the hair to stand on end in reaction to cold or emotional stimuli.

**Nails** are hard, keratinized cells that protect the ends of the digits and assist us in grasping; the nail grows from the **lunula** (crescent-shaped white area at base of nail).

**Sebaceous (Oil) glands** connect to the hair follicles and produce an oily substance called **sebum** that prevent dehydration, soften the skin and hair, and slow the growth of bacteria.

**Sweat glands** known as **sudoriferous** glands are found in most areas of the body; most are located on the forehead, armpits, soles of the feet, and palms of the hands; two main types are **eccrine** and **apocrine** glands.

***Eccrine glands*** are the most common and are responsible for the moisture that appears on the surface of the body when the temperature rises, particularly during physical activity; the functions of the eccrine glands are to cool the body and provide minor elimination of metabolic waste.

***Apocrine glands*** are located in areas of body hair; discharge their secretions when a person is under stress; the secretion is thicker and has a stronger odor; located in the axillary and anogenital areas.

***Ceruminous glands*** are modified apocrine glands found in the external ear and secrete **cerumen** (earwax).

## The Effects of Aging on the Integumentary System

Collagen and elastin network of the skin tends to lose its elasticity.

Sebaceous glands produce less sebum to moisturize the skin.

The skin becomes thinner, drier, and more prone to growths.

Swelling (edema) of tissues can appear around and under the eyes.

## Immune & Lymphatic

The **Immune system** consists of a complex array of organs, cells, and molecules distributed throughout the body to keep people safe from a variety of "foreign" invaders and diseases.

### Components of the Immune System

**Tonsils** located strategically under the epithelial lining of the oral cavity and pharynx produce **lymphocytes** to defend against invading bacteria.

**Thymus** is important in the development and maturation of certain **lymphocytes** and in programming them to become **T cells** of the immune system.

**Lymph nodes** are small masses of lymph tissue in which lymphocytes are produced; positioned strategically to protect the respiratory and gastrointestinal tracts from microbes and other foreign material.

**Lymph vessels (lymphatics)** carry lymph fluid, nutrients, and waste material between the body tissues and bloodstream; lymph nodes filter lymph fluid as it flows through them trapping bacteria, viruses, and other foreign substances which are destroyed by lymphocytes.

**Bone marrow** produces white blood cells (**lymphocytes**), which are transported through the blood and lymph.

**Spleen** is the largest of lymphoid organs, located near the stomach under the diaphragm; **macrophages** in the spleen filter out worn-out red blood cells and destroy microorganisms in the blood; it stores **lymphocytes** and releases them as part of the immune response.

**White corpuscles** (white blood cells) also called **leukocytes** are produced in the spleen, lymph nodes, and the red marrow of bones; the most important function is to protect the body against disease by combating different infectious and toxic agents that can invade the body; most **leukocytes** engulf and digest harmful bacteria and other foreign materials in a process called **phagocytosis**.

### The Mechanisms of Nonspecific Resistance to Disease (Immunity)

<u>**Nonspecific/Innate Immunity**</u>: Present at birth, consisting of many nonspecific factors and blood-based immunity from the mother.

**Skin** – Sebaceous glands produce **sebum** which functions to waterproof the skin; thought to have antibacterial action.

**Mouth** – lined with a tough **mucous membrane** irrigated constantly by a back flow of saliva; **saliva** contains an enzyme called **lysozyme** that is antibacterial and mucus that contains **immunoglobulin A**, an antibody.

**Stomach** – **hydrochloric acid** produced by the stomach lining has a **low pH (acidic/base)** to kill most organisms entering the body with food or drink or by being swallowed.

**Intestines** – rely on the bactericidal action of the stomach; intestines are supplied liberally with lymphatic tissue throughout their length.

**Respiratory Tract** – hairs in the nose prevent insects & large particles from entering the upper respiratory tract; **Nasal mucosa** secretes mucus that traps smaller particles (bactericidal & virucidal properties); **lysozyme** is present in nasal secretions.

**Trachea & Lungs** – lined with a ciliated mucous membrane, serves to trap any organisms that may have escaped the upper tract; **alveolar macrophages phagocytose** any organisms that reach the **alveoli**; lymph nodes act as another filter.

**Genitourinary Tract** – constant downward flow of urine through the ureter and bladder tends to protect against ascending infections; resident flora of the vagina, especially **lactobacillus**, helps to maintain an acid environment, creating an inhospitable habitat for invading pathogens.

**Eye** – tears produced by **lacrimal glands** constantly irrigate the surface of the eyeball; tears contain **lysozyme** that forms an effective barrier against infection.

**Ear** – **Cerumen** or ear wax provides a sticky barrier to foreign agents entering the ear canal.

## The Mechanisms of Specific Immunity

**Specific** or **Acquired Immunity** is the result of an encounter with a new substance, which triggers events that induce an immune response specific against that particular substance.

**Lymphocytes** are the cells specific to immunity because they can recognize and destroy specific molecules (**B-lymphocytes**, **T-lymphocytes** and **macrophages**).

Whenever **T-cells** and **B-cells** are activated, some of the cells become memory cells.

The lymphocyte pattern set up with the first infection can respond to a second exposure and prevent infection.

**Lymphocytes** use three ways to fight infection:

1. Elimination of extracellular microorganisms.

2. Elimination of microorganisms that normally survive for long periods in macrophages.

3. Elimination of microorganisms that infect cells without an endogenous antimicrobial defense system.

## The Relationship of the Immune System to Other Body Systems

**Immunity** is a bodywide process:

**Integumentary System** – provides a mechanical barrier.

**Skeletal System** – provides the bone marrow as the developmental home for the lymphocytes and macrophages.

**Muscular System** – heat from the muscular system actively initiates feverlike effects.

**Nervous& Endocrine Systems** – directly interact through a shared chemical language.

**Cardiovascular System** – provides the travel network, lymphatic system, and filtering system.

**Respiratory System** – provides oxygen needed by immune cells, and secretes acids hostile to pathogens.

**Urinary System** – eliminates waste and maintains the protective acid balance.

**Reproductive System** – works with the endocrine system to influence the process through hormone function.

**Lymphatic** – the lymphatic system acts as an aid to and is interlinked with, the blood-vascular system.

## The Function and Formation of Lymph

**Lymph** is a straw-colored fluid derived from the blood and interstitial fluid.

**Lymph** acts as a medium of exchange, trading to the cells its nutritive materials and receiving in return the waste products of metabolism.

**Lymph** carries plasma proteins to the bloodstream and transports absorbed fats from the small intestine to the bloodstream.

## Lymphatic Vessels, Major Lymphatic Vessels, & Direction of Lymph Flow

**Lymphatic Vessels** begin with the network of lymph capillaries that are located throughout the body; the **lymphatic capillary** network drains tissue fluid from nearly all tissues and organs that have a blood vascularization.

The moment fluid enters a **lymph capillary**; a flap valve prevents it from returning into interstitial spaces.

**Lymph capillaries** join to form larger lymph vessels that look like veins.

The large vessels continue to merge and become two **major lymphatic vessels**, the **right lymphatic duct** and the **thoracic duct** (left lymphatic duct).

**Right lymphatic duct** drains lymph from the right side of head, neck, chest, and right arm and empties into the right subclavian vein.

**Thoracic duct** drains lymph from the legs, left arm, left side of head, neck, and chest and empties into the **left subclavian vein**.

The direction of lymph flow is toward the heart (**centripetal**).

# Muscular

## Types and Functions of Muscle Tissue and Fascia

### Movement

**Voluntary**, **striated**, or **skeletal** muscles are controlled by conscious will; are attached to your bones, which allow you to walk or wave your hands.

**Involuntary**, **nonstriated** or **smooth** muscles are controlled by the autonomic nervous system; found on organ walls such as the intestine; contractions produce movement of food through the intestine.

**Cardiac** or **heart** muscle is only found in the heart; it is striated like skeletal muscle; produces the pumping of the blood in the heart and throughout the body.

### Stability

Muscle holds your bones together to stabilize joints.

Small muscles hold your vertebrae together and stabilize your spinal column.

### Controlling of openings and passages

Muscles form valve like structures called sphincters.

Sphincters control movement of substances in and out of passages.

The urethral sphincter prevents or allows urination.

### Heat production

When muscles contract heat is released.

This helps the body maintain a normal temperature.

Moving your body can make you warmer if you're cold.

**Fascia** organizes muscles into functional groups, surrounds each individual muscle, extends inward throughout the muscle creating bundles, and eventually surrounds each muscle fiber.

**Superficial fascia** is situated just below the skin and covers the entire muscular system.

The **Epimysium** is the layer of fascia that closely covers an individual muscle.

The **Perimysium** extends inward from the epimysium and separates the muscle into bundles of muscle fibers or **fascicles**.

The **Endomysium** is the delicate connective tissue covering each muscle fiber has within the fascicle.

A **Tendon** is a fibrous connective tissue band that attaches muscle to bone; transfers muscle contraction to bones or other tissues to produce movement.

An **Aponeurosis** is a broad flat sheet of fibrous connective tissue that attaches muscle tissue to bones or other tissues.

## The Anatomy of Skeletal Muscle Fibers

Skeletal muscle fibers are long, cylindric, tapered cells that have cross-striations by the contractile structure inside.

The **Sarcolemma** is the plasma membrane that covers muscle cells; numerous nuclei lie beneath the sarcolemma.

The **Sarcoplasm** of a muscle fiber is similar to the cytoplasm of other cells, but contains large amounts of stored glycogen and an oxygen binding protein called myoglobin.

**Myoglobin** is a red pigment similar to hemoglobin that stores oxygen within the muscle cells.

**Sarcomeres** are structural units of contraction in skeletal muscle fibers.

**Myofibrils**, which are chains of sarcomeres, are packed side by side with the sarcoplasm.

**The functional units of skeletal muscles** are small portions of myofibrils, and each myofibril is a chain of sarcomere units laid end to end.

The **neuromuscular** or **myoneural junction** is the site where the muscle fiber and nerve fiber meet; a motor unit is a motor neuron and all the muscle fibers it controls.

**Anaerobic respiration** is a process in which glucose is broken down in the absence of oxygen; results in the formation of **lactic acid**.

**Aerobic respiration** is a **catabolic** process where oxygen is needed and stored by muscle cells in **myoglobin**.

**Anabolism** is a process of building up of larger molecules from smaller ones.

**Catabolism** is the breaking down of larger substances into smaller ones.

**Hypertonic muscles** involve muscles or groups of muscles that seem tight or result in a postural deviation or constriction in joint movement, or both.

When a muscle is tight and overactive, it is common for the **antagonist** (the muscle responsible for the opposite movement) to be flaccid, weak, or **hypotonic**.

**Hypotonic muscles** often indicate the opposing muscle (**antagonist**) or the synergistic muscles are found to be tight, overactive, or **hypertonic**.

## Types of Skeletal Muscle Fibers

**Type I**, **slow twitch** (red) **fibers**, contract more slowly and have a high resistance to fatigue; they contain large amounts of myoglobin and are classified as aerobic because they require oxygen for contraction.

**Type II**, **fast twitch** (white) **fibers**, contract more rapidly and forcefully (5x-10x faster); they depend on creatine phosphate and glycogen for ATP generation and they fatigue quickly.

**Intermediate fibers (Type IIa)** combine the qualities of slow twitch and fast twitch fibers to provide a rapid, moderately forceful contraction with moderate fatigue resistance.

# Nervous

The **sympathetic** and **parasympathetic** nervous systems work together to maintain homeostasis.

**Homeostasis** is the maintenance of a relatively constant internal environment suitable for the survival of body cells and tissues.

**Neuroglia** is specialized connective tissue cells that support, protect, and hold neurons together.

**Neuron** or **nerve cell** is the structural unit of the nervous system; it consists of a cell body and its nerve fibers; **dendrites**, which look like small hairs, connect with other neurons to receive information; **axons** conducts impulses away from the cell body; axons are covered by a **myelin sheath**, made of fatty **Schwann cells**, that insulates the nerve and aids in the conduction of the nerve impulse.

Small gaps between segments of myelin sheath are called **nodes of Ranvier** and help speed the nerve impulses.

**Sensory (afferent) nerves** collect information from the body and transmit it in the form of electrical impulses to the CNS for action.

**Motor (efferent) nerves** cause movement through the action of muscles.

**Mixed (afferent/efferent) nerves** consist of both sensory and motor nerves.

The **CNS (Central Nervous System)** consists of the brain and spinal cord; it is responsible for our thoughts and emotions, for receiving and interpreting incoming sensory information, for disseminating appropriate motor responses to maintain safety and homeostasis.

The **PNS (Peripheral Nervous System)** consists of all the nerves that connect the CNS to the rest of the body; it includes: the cranial and spinal nerves and all of their branches; it is divided into:

**Autonomic Nervous System**: connect the CNS to the visceral organs such as the heart, blood vessels, glands, and intestines; subdivided into sympathetic and parasympathetic nervous systems.

**Sympathetic Nervous System** supplies the glands, involuntary muscles of internal organs, and walls of blood vessels with nerves and prepares the body for energy-expending circumstances; fight or flight response.

**Parasympathetic Nervous System** functions to conserve energy and reverse the action of the sympathetic nervous system; reduced heart rate, respiration and blood pressure, and increased digestion and elimination.

**Somatic Nervous System**: involves those nerves connecting the CNS, the skeletal muscles, and skin.

### The Brain and Protective Coverings

The **Cerebrum** is the largest portion of the brain; presides over speech, sensation, communication, memory, reasoning, will, and emotions; cerebrum is divided into left and right hemispheres.

The **Cerebellum** is the smaller part of the brain located below the cerebrum and at the back of the cranium; helps to maintain body balance, coordinates voluntary muscles, and makes muscular movement smooth and graceful.

The **Diencephalon** is found between the cerebrum and midbrain; it contains the thalamus, hypothalamus, pineal, and pituitary glands.

The **Thalamus** is a relay center for sensory information coming into the brain; it is associated with pain, temperature, crude touch, and reflex muscle coordination.

The **Hypothalamus** regulates and coordinates functions such as heart rate, blood pressure, peristaltic actions, appetite and satiety, pleasure, temperature, and general coordination of ANS functions.

The **Pineal gland** is found on the dorsal side of the diencephalon; it functions as an internal biologic clock that regulates daily activities (**circadian rhythms**) and yearly (**circannual rhythms**); exposure to sunlight assists these functions; the pineal gland needs darkness to convert serotonin to melatonin; **melatonin** triggers the pituitary gland to release luteinizing hormone and is involved in the sleep pattern.

The **Pituitary gland** (**master gland**) hormones, governed by the hypothalamus, control other endocrine glands.

**The brain stem has three parts**:

The **Midbrain** contains reflex centers for visual and auditory stimuli and correlates information about muscle tone and posture.

The **Pons**, located between the midbrain and medulla oblongata, assists in the coordinated patterns of breathing, eye movement, and facial expressions and is involved in rapid eye movement (REM) sleep.

The **Medulla oblongata** is an enlarged continuation of the spinal cord that regulates movements of the heart and control vasoconstriction of the arteries and the rate and depth of respiration

The **meninges** is a special connective tissue membrane that has **three layers**:

**Dura mater (tough mother)** is the outer layer of the Meninges covering the brain and spinal cord.

**Arachnoid mater (spider layer)** is the middle space of the meninges; provides a space for the blood vessels and the circulation of the spinal fluid.

**Pia mater (delicate mother)**, the innermost layer of the meninges, is attached to the surface of the brain and spinal cord and is richly supplied with blood vessels to nourish underlying tissues.

### The 12 Cranial Nerves: Name, Location, and Function

1. **Olfactory nerve**, located in the nose; sense of smell.

2. **Optic nerve**, located in retina of eye; sense of sight.

3. **Oculomotor nerve**, located in muscles of eye; controls eye movements.

4. **Trochlear nerve**, located superior oblique muscle of eye; rotates eyeball downward and outward.

5. **Trigeminal nerve**, located in face, teeth, and tongue; controls sensations of the face and movements of the jaw and tongue.

6. **Abducent nerve**, located in recti muscles of the eye; rotates eyeball outward.

7. **Facial nerve**, located in face and neck; controls facial muscles of expression and some muscles of the neck and ear.

8. **Auditory nerve**, located in ear; sense of hearing.

9. **Glossopharyngeal nerve**, located in tongue and pharynx; sense of taste.

10. **Vagus nerve**, located in pharynx, larynx, heart, lungs, and digestive organs; controls sensations and muscular movements relating to talking, heart action, breathing, and digestion.

11. **Spinal accessory nerve**, located in shoulder; controls movement of neck muscles.

12. **Hypoglossal nerve**, located in tongue and neck; controls movement of tongue.

### Spinal Nerves & Branches of the Cervical, Brachial, Lumbar, & Sacral Plexuses

**Thirty-one** pairs of spinal nerves; contain both sensory and motor nerve fibers for two-way communication between the CNS and body; spinal nerve anterior root contains motor neurons and posterior root contains sensory neurons.

**Eight** pairs of cervical nerves; the **Cervical plexus** consists of the four upper cervical nerves that supply the skin and control the movement of the head, neck, and shoulders.

**Twelve** pairs of thoracic nerves; the **Brachial plexus** is composed of four lower cervical nerves and the first pair of thoracic nerves that control arm movement.

**Five** pairs of lumbar nerves; the **Lumbar plexus** is formed from the first four lumbar nerves which supply the skin, the abdominal organs, hip, thigh, knee, and leg.

**Five** pairs of sacral nerves; the **Sacral plexus** is formed from the fourth and fifth lumbar nerves, and the first four sacral nerves.

**One** pair of coccygeal nerves; the **Coccygeal plexus** is formed from a portion of the fourth sacral nerves, the fifth sacral nerve, and the coccygeal nerve.

**Dermatomes** are areas of the skin supplied by a single spinal nerve; knowing the dermatome pattern enables a clinician to locate injuries in the spinal cord and spinal nerves.

A **Reflex arc** is the pathway the nerve impulse follows from the receptor through sensory neurons to the spinal cord or brain, back through motor neurons to the effector action; a **reflex** is a fast automatic response to a stimulus that helps maintain homeostasis, which includes a sensory and motor nerve.

## Somatic reflexes

The **Stretch reflex** is a homeostatic mechanism that prevents muscle trauma in response to a sudden or intense stretch.

The **Tendon reflex** also known as the **inverse stretch reflex**, is a feedback mechanism that controls muscle tension by allowing for muscle relaxation.

The **Flexor reflex** is a withdrawal reflex that begins with stimulation of the sensory receptor, often by something painful like stepping on a nail or contact with a hot flame.

The **Crossed extensor reflex** works in coordination with the flexor reflex.

## Sensory receptors

**Mechanoreceptors** respond to mechanical stimulation such as touch, pressure, vibration, and stretch; examples include **Ruffini end organs**, **Pacini corpuscles**, and **Merkel disks** in the skin and the **proprioceptors** located in muscle, fascia, and joints.

**Thermoreceptors** are located in the skin and mouth; detect heat and cold.

**Photoreceptors** are located in the retina of the eyes, rods, and cones are sensitive to light and detect color.

**Chemoreceptors** located in the mouth and nose, are sensitive to certain chemical stimuli and give us the sense of taste and smell; chemoreceptors in certain arteries are sensitive to carbon dioxide and pH changes.

**Nociceptors** detect pain and are located in nearly every tissue in the body except the brain.

## Synapses and Neurotransmitters

**Synapse** is the junction where nerve signals jump from one nerve to another; the space between two neurons or a neuron and an effector organ.

**Neurotransmitter** is a chemical that sends a nerve signal across a synapse; major neurotransmitters (stimulatory and inhibitory):

**Acetylcholine** stimulates the skeletal muscles and primarily acts on the parasympathetic nervous system; can stimulate or inhibit various organs; plentiful in the brain, the chemical is involved in memory.

**Catecholamines** are involved in sleep, motor function, mood, and pleasure.

**Epinephrine** can be a stimulant or inhibitor; found in several areas of the CNS and sympathetic divisions of ANS; involved in fight-or-flight responses such as dilation of blood vessels to the skeletal muscles; classified as a hormone when secreted by the adrenal gland.

**Norepinephrine** can excite or inhibit; found in the CNS (especially the hypothalamus and limbic system) and sympathetic division of the ANS; causes constriction of blood vessels, is considered a "feel good" neurotransmitter and is involved in emotional responses.

**Dopamine** is generally excitatory; found in the brain and ANS; a feel-good neurotransmitter is involved in emotions and moods and in the regulation of motor control and the executive functioning of the brain.

**Histamine** is considered a stimulant; released by the mast cells as part of the inflammatory process; causes itching at the cellular level and also works as a vasodilator; found in the hypothalamus, the chemical regulates body temperature and water balance and plays a role in our emotions.

**Serotonin** usually works as an inhibitor in the CNS and is synthesized into melatonin and affects our biological cycles, sleep, and moods.

# Reproduction

The continuation of the species is the biologic function of the reproductive system; the essence of reproduction is the duality of yin/yang and male/female, when at the moment of conception two cells create one whole.

## The Male Reproductive System

The functions of the male reproductive system are the production of sperm, the production of male hormones (testosterone), and the performance of the sex act.

**Testicles (Testes)** are two small, egg-shaped glands enclosed in an external sac called the scrotum; tiny **seminiferous tubules** in the testicles produce sperm in a process called **spermatogenesis**.

**Epididymis** located in the scrotum, receives sperm from the testes and stores the sperm until it becomes fully mature.

**Vas deferens** is where the sperm collects until it is expelled from the body.

**Seminal vesicles** are two convoluted, glandular tubes located on each side of the prostate that produce a nutritious fluid that is excreted into the ejaculatory ducts at the time of emission.

**Prostate gland** lies below the urinary bladder and surrounds the first part of the urethra; it secretes an alkaline fluid that enhances the sperm's ability to swim; the fluid also neutralizes the acidic vaginal secretions, protecting the sperm and increasing its chances of reaching and fertilizing the ovum.

**Cowper's (bulbourethral) glands** are two pea-sized glands located beneath the prostate that produce mucus that serve to lubricate the urethra.

**Urethra** serves to convey urine from the bladder and to carry reproductive cells and secretions out of the body.

**Penis** is the male organ of copulation, consisting of erectile tissue that can become engorged and erect to deposit the sperm-containing semen.

## The Female Reproductive System

The functions of the female reproductive system are to produce the ovum and female hormones, to receive sperm during the sex act, and to carry the growing fetus during pregnancy.

**Ovaries (female gonads)** are a pair of glandular organs located within the pelvic area; they produce **ovum**, the egg cell capable of being fertilized by a **spermatozoon** and developing into a new life; they produce the female hormones **estrogen** and **progesterone**.

**Fallopian tubes (oviducts)** are the egg-carrying tubes of the female reproductive system; they extend from the uterus to the ovaries.

**Uterus** is a pear-shaped, muscular organ consisting of an upper portion, the body, and the cervix or neck; during pregnancy it expands to accommodate the fetus and a large amount of fluid.

**Vagina** is a muscular tube or canal leading from the **vulva** (external part of female reproductive system) opening to the cervix and is the lower part of the birth canal; the vagina is the organ that receives the penis and the ejaculated semen.

**Pregnancy** or **gestation** is the physiologic condition that occurs from the time an ovum is fertilized until childbirth.

**Fertilization** is the penetration of the egg by a sperm.

The **ovum** contains one X chromosome; sperm contains an X or Y chromosome; the male determines the sex of the baby.

If a male sperm (Y) reaches the egg, a male baby results; if a female sperm (X) reaches the egg, a female baby results.

**Gestation** takes approximately 280 days or 40 weeks; divided into three trimesters.

## First trimester

Radical hormonal changes influence mood, digestion, sleep, and energy levels.

Actual menstruation stops; as the uterus begins to enlarge and press down on the bladder, the urge to urinate occurs more frequently.

Developing milk glands and the increased blood supply to the breasts makes them sensitive; nipples enlarge and become more erect; areolae darken and become broader.

Fatigue is a major symptom; it continues until the fourteenth to twentieth week of pregnancy; about 10 hours of sleep is suggested.

Progesterone relaxes the smooth muscles of the digestive tract slowing down the digestive process and leading to constipation.

60% to 80% of women suffer nausea and vomiting.

## Second trimester

Appetite increases, blood volume increases, and the body places additional workload on all physiologic functions.

Increase blood in the vaginal area causes an increase in vaginal secretions or discharge; a foul odor or itching or a yellow or green discharge may indicate a vaginal infection.

Progesterone depresses the CNS and may cause moodiness and depression.

By week 15 the baby weighs almost 2ounces; the bones are growing and muscle movement is increasing; a soft, fine hair called lanugo covers the baby.

By 21 weeks the baby weighs about 1 lb and is nearly 10 to 11 inches long; nerve cells that allow the baby's brain to receive and transmit messages are forming layers in the brain.

By the end of week 21, the layers of retina are developed and the skin is developing a white coating called vernix caseosa, a fatty film that protects the baby's skin from breakdown in the amniotic fluid.

Gallbladder takes a longer time to empty, allowing bile salts to accumulate that causes itching.

At the end of the second trimester, hearing is completely developed; the baby's senses are functioning at a higher level.

Some edema is normal in pregnancy, but edema all over the body a serious problem requiring referral to a physician.

## Third trimester

Begins after about 26 weeks of pregnancy; these last 3 months are critical to the development of organs such as the lungs and brain.

Baby is about 15 inches long and weighs about 3 lbs; may suck thumb, hiccup and respond to stimuli.

Colostrum, the early form of milk may leak from breasts.

By month 8 the baby is about 18 inches and weighs about 5 lb; lungs are still immature and the brain develops rapidly; baby shifts into a position it will maintain until birth.

By 36 weeks, the baby is about 20 inches long and weighs about 6 to 7 lb and will gain about ½ lb per week until delivery; the lungs are mature.

## Birth

**Oxytocin** stimulates contraction of the uterus, causes delivery of the placenta after expulsion of the fetus, and promotes parental bonding.

**Prelabor** can begin anywhere in the last few weeks or days of pregnancy; diarrhea may occur as a way of emptying the intestinal tract before actual labor begins; **Braxton Hicks** contractions may be frequent (these are painless).

As the baby's head presses down against the amniotic membranes containing fluid, the membranes may break ("breaking water"); fluid is normally clear and odorless.

**Early labor** is characterized by contractions that cause the cervix to dilate 3 to 4 cm; these contractions are wavelike, last 30 to 45 seconds and occur anywhere from 5 to 20 minutes apart.

**Active labor** lasts about 3 to 5 hours; contractions occur every 2 to 4 minutes and last up to 60 seconds; an **epidural**, a painkiller that numbs from the breasts down may be given; an extreme urge to push and rectal pressure is felt.

**Transition phase** proceeds to delivery and lasts from 30 to 90 minutes; contractions are intense, occurring every 30 seconds and lasting 90 seconds.

**Delivery** is where the woman actually gets to push; as the head emerges, the mother may feel intense stinging and burning sensations; an **episiotomy**, makes an incision in the perineum, the area between the vagina and rectum to enlarge the opening for vaginal births.

**Cesarean section** or **C-section** is a surgical procedure that is essentially abdominal delivery.

# Respiratory

**Respiration** is the exchange of carbon dioxide and oxygen that takes place at three levels in the body:

**External respiration** is the exchange between the external environment and the blood and takes place in the lungs.

**Internal respiration** is the gaseous exchange between the blood and the cells of the body.

**Cellular respiration** or **oxidation** occurs within the cell.

## Structures of the Respiratory System

<u>Upper respiratory tract</u> consists of the nasal cavity, all its structures and the pharynx.

The **Nasal cavity** consists of an irregular cavity divided by a septum; it is the first of the respiratory passages through which incoming air passes; its function is to ensure that the air is warmed, moistened, and filtered.

The **Pharynx** is a cone shaped tube common to the respiratory and digestive systems; commonly called the throat; air is warmed and moistened.

<u>Lower respiratory tract</u> consists of the larynx, trachea, and bronchi and alveoli in the lungs.

The **Larynx** is composed of several irregularly shaped cartilages; commonly known as the voice box; filters, moistens, and warms air; voice production via the vocal cords; airway is closed during swallowing by the epiglottis.

The **Trachea** is the tube that extends from the larynx to the bronchi; it is the passageway through which air passes to the lungs.

The **Bronchi** begin where the trachea branches; within the lungs, the bronchi divides into smaller tubes called bronchioles; bronchioles subdivide into microscopic tubes called alveolar ducts.

**Alveoli** are air sacs surrounded by capillaries where internal respiration takes place.

The **Lungs** lie in the thoracic cavity; the **right lung** has **three lobes** and the **left lung** has **two lobes**; lungs allow the free exchange of gases to take place between the alveoli and the capillary network that surround them.

## Respiratory Rates

The respiratory rate in adults is about 12 to 16 breaths per minute; a newborn is about 35, gradually decreasing to adult values by age 20.

Fear, grief, and shock slow the rate.

Excitement, anger, and sexual arousal increase the respiratory rate.

Changing in breathing rates can occur as a result of increased oxygen requirement from exercise, in obesity as a result of vessel resistance, during infections and fever because of increased energy requirements, in heart failure from decreased oxygen flow and during pain because of increased nervous stimulation.

# Skeletal

**The Skeletal System has five main functions**:

1. To offer framework that supports body structures and gives shape to the body.

2. To protect delicate internal organs and tissues.

3. To provide attachments for muscles and act as levers in conjunction with muscles to produce movement.

4. To manufacture blood cells in the red bone marrow.

5. To store minerals such as calcium phosphate, calcium carbonate, magnesium and sodium.

## Parts of a Long Bone:

The **Epiphysis** is an enlarged area on the ends of long bones that articulates with other bones.

**Articular cartilage** is a layer of hyaline cartilage covering the end surface of the epiphysis; it is the shock-absorbing surface where two bones meet to form a joint.

The **Diaphysis** is the bone shaft between the epiphysis.

The **Periosteum** is a fibrous membrane that functions to protect the bone and serves as an attachment of tendons and ligaments; contains nerves, blood, and lymph vessels and is essential to bone nutrition and repair.

**Compact bone tissue** forms the hard bone found in the shafts of long bones and along the outside of flat bones.

**Cancellous bone** or **spongy bone** is located inside long bones and flat bones, consists of irregularly shaped spaces defined by thin, bony plates; filled with red bone marrow and is the site of production for blood cells.

The **Medullary cavity** is a hollow chamber formed in the shaft of long bones that is filled with yellow bone marrow.

The **Marrow** is the connective tissue filling in the cavities of bones that forms red and white blood cells.

## Types of Fractures and the Process of Fracture Repair:

**Incomplete (Greenstick)** – has a small slender crack in the bone.

**Closed (Simple)** – the broken bone has not pierced the skin.

**Compound (Open)** – the broken bone pierces through the skin.

**Comminuted** – the bone is shattered into small pieces.

Fractured bones are treated by **reduction**, which means that a physician pulls the broken ends into alignment to establish continuity of the bone. Bone usually heals after being immobilized by either a cast or by surgically implanted pins, plates, or screws. Fracture healing has five stages: hematoma formation, cellular proliferation, callus formation, ossification, and remodeling.

## The Effects of Aging and Exercise on Bone (mass) Tissue

As we age, various changes occur in the skeleton:

Loss of calcium begins earlier in women than in men.

The bone matrix is not replaced as quickly because the body produces less protein; this may lead to brittle bones (**osteoporosis**).

Bone fractures heal slowly in elderly persons.

Beginning at age 40, the intervertebral disks begin to thin, and the average person loses a half an inch of height every 20 years.

**Resistance training** is very likely to have a positive effect on bone tissue; resistance training may lead to decreased risk for osteoporosis, fractures, and falls consequences of loss of bone mass.

## Classification of Bones:

**Flat bones** are found in the skull, ribs, and pelvis.

**Long bones** are found in the arms and legs.

**Short bones** are shaped like long bones, but are much smaller; hands, fingers, feet, and toes.

**Irregular bones** are found in the vertebrae and scapula.

**Sesamoid bones** such as the patella.

**Cube-shaped bones** are found in wrist bones (**carpals**) and ankle bones (**tarsals**).

## Bones of the Axial Skeleton:

**Cranium** (8) - encloses and protects the brain: frontal (1), parietal (2), occipital (1), temporal (2), sphenoid (1), ethmoid (1).

**Face** (14) – forms the structure of the eyes, nose, cheeks, mouth, and jaws: maxilla (2), palatine (2), zygomatic (2), lacrimal (2), nasal (2), vomer (1), inferior nasal concha (2), mandible (1).

**Ear** or **Ossicles** (6) – form the internal structure of the ears: malleus (2), incus (2), stapes (2).

**Hyoid** (1) – supports the base of the tongue.

**Vertebral column** (26) – forms the spinal column, which supports the head and trunk, protects the spinal cord and provides attachment for the ribs: cervical vertebrae (7), thoracic vertebrae (12), lumbar vertebrae (5), sacrum (1), and coccyx (1).

**Thoracic cage** (25) – ribs/costals (24 or 12 pair) forms a protective cage for the lungs and heart, sternum (1) serves as an attachment for the ribs at the front of the chest.

## Bones of the Appendicular Skeleton:

**Upper extremities** (64) – clavicle (2), scapula (2), humerus (2), ulna (2), radius (2), carpals (16), metacarpals (10), phalanges (28).

**Lower extremities** (66) – pelvis (fusion of three bones: the ischium, pubis, and ilium) (6), femur (2), patella (2), tibia (2), fibula (2), tarsals (14), metatarsals (10), phalanges (28).

## Bone Structures

**Bony Landmarks** often serve as regions for muscle attachment or provide passage or space for nerves and vessels.

## Depressions and Openings:

**Canal**: a tunnel or tube in bone.

**Fissure**: a groove or slit between two bones.

**Foramen**: an opening in a bone.

**Fossa**: a shallow depression in the surface or at the end of a bone.

**Groove**: a depression in a bone that holds blood vessels, nerves, or tendons.

**Meatus**: a tunnel or canal found in a bone.

**Notch**: an indentation or large groove.

**Sinus**: an air cavity within a bone.

## Processes That Form Joints:

**Condyle**: a rounded, knuckle-like prominence, usually at a point of articulation

**Head**: a rounded articulating process at the end of a bone

**Facet**: a smooth, flat surface

**Process**: any prominent, bony growth that projects

**Trochlea**: a pulley-shaped structure

**<u>Processes to Which Tendons and Ligaments Attach</u>**:

**Crest**: a ridge on a bone.

**Epicondyle**: a projection above a condyle.

**Line**: a ridge that is smaller than a crest.

**Spine** or **spinous process**: a sharp slender projection.

**Trochanter**: a large process for muscle attachment.

**Tubercle**: a small, rounded process.

**Tuberosity**: a large rounded process.

*Osteoclasts* are large cells that dissolve bone; they come from the bone marrow and are related to white blood cells.

*Osteoblasts* are the cells that form new bone.

*Osteocytes* are mature osteoblasts that have become trapped within the very bone matrix they produced.

*Sprain* is an injury to a joint resulting in stretching or tearing of the ligaments.

*Strain* is the tearing of muscle tissue or tendons.

## Special Senses

### Hearing

Vibrations in the air are taken in by the external ear, called the **auricle** or **pinna**, and funneled into the **external auditory meatus**, which leads to the middle ear.

Inside the middle ear, the sounds reach the **tympanic membrane** or **eardrum**; as the eardrum vibrates in response, it pulls on the tiny bones called **ossicles** to amplify the sounds.

The motion transfers to the **malleus** (hammer), which hits the **incus** (anvil), which pulls on the **stapes** (stirrup); this bone rests on the oval window, a membrane at the beginning of the inner ear.

The **eustachian** (auditory) **tube** connects the middle ear with the throat and equalizes pressure between the middle ear and outside air; yawning, swallowing, or chewing helps to open the tube to relieve pressure.

Sound waves leave the middle ear and travel to the inner ear, where the **cochlea**, a spiral shell, is the center of our hearing; the inner ear has three canals, the outer two carry the amplified vibrations.

The sound waves travel through a thin membrane to the middle canal, the **organ of Corti**; in this region, fluid-filled circular ducts are positioned at right angles to each other, and each duct contains hair cells embedded in a gelatinous substance; these specialized receptor cells respond to vibrations and motion.

The directional hair cells transfer information about our head position and speed of movement; this sensory information is transformed into electrical signals, which the auditory nerve conducts to the brain.

Disruption of this proprioceptive mechanism often results in balance problems or **vertigo**.

### Vision

The eyeball is a fluid-filled sphere composed of three layers. Vision occurs when light rays enter through the lens and are focused on the retina.

The **outer layer** comprises the sclera and the cornea; the **sclera** is a white, fibrous structure that maintains the shape of the eye and protects the inner structures; the **cornea** is the clear portion in the front that allows light to enter the eye.

The **middle layer** contains the ciliary body, choroid, and iris; the **ciliary body**, on the anterior portion, contains smooth muscles attached to the lens by ligaments; the **choroid**, which covers the posterior of the sclera, is filled with capillaries to nourish the eye.

The cells of the choroid contain **melanin** and absorb light as it enters the eye; the **iris**, the colored portion of the eye, contains smooth muscles and controls the size of the pupil, which increases or decreases the amount of light allowed to enter the eye.

The **inner layer** of the eyeball is the **retina**, which contains photoreceptor cells and neurons; the **rods**, take in information about the levels of lightness and darkness and are responsible for recognizing shapes and patterns and providing contrast.

**Cones** of the retina help us identify color and brightness; **rods** and **cones** receive the mechanical signals, transform them into chemical substances, and create an electrical signal that is sent to the brain via the **optic nerve**.

Vision signals are organized and processed in our **cerebral cortex**; information received from the left and right eyes converge in the **visual cortex**; signals received when we are not paying attention are sent to the **posterior parietal cortex**; all three areas work to process and coordinate visual information.

Six muscles control movement of the eyeball; **lacrimal glands** produce tears that keep our eyeballs moist, fight infections, and remove foreign particles.

## Taste

Specific areas on the tongue correspond to four distinct tastes – sweet, sour, salty, and bitter.

Molecules of food bind to receptor sites on the tongue, cheeks, and floor of the mouth; the rest of our tasting is done through our sense of smell.

On average, an adult has more than 10,000 taste buds, which usually last about 10 days, are not replaced as frequently.

Our individual preferences for certain tastes may be because of cultural differences or genetics; bitter tastes are the most easily identified.

## Smell

The actual activity of **olfaction** or smell involves chemical receptors found in the roof of the nasal cavity.

As an odor makes contact with the receptors, they transform chemical signals into electrical signals and transmit them to the temporal lobes of the brain.

The smell centers of the brain are connected with the limbic system and thus have an emotional and behavioral effect.

Blocked nasal passages affect the senses of smell and taste.

Each of us has a unique body odor that changes in response to our emotions; we can smell fear, danger, anger, and sexual arousal.

The nerves from the nose end in the olfactory bulb in the limbic area of the brain, the portion of the brain that also controls much of our autonomic, involuntary actions.

## Touch

The skin is the most sensitive of our organs and is the home for touch receptors of the nervous system.

Touch is the first sense to develop in the embryo.

Touch is our most important and yet the most neglected of our senses; without the ability to feel, we are in constant danger.

A lack of touch, especially in infants, the elderly, and those with weakened immune systems, can be life threatening and contribute to a condition called **maramus** (wasting away).

Touch deprivation leads to a reduced production of the neuroendocrine chemicals necessary for well-being.

Millions of sensory receptors in the skin alert us to danger through variations in temperature, vibration, and pressure; touch informs us of differences in texture, shape, resistance, and tension.

About one third of the 5 million or so sensory receptors are in the skin of our hands; the fingertips have more than 1000 nerve endings per square inch, and the lips and tongue have even more.

# Urinary

The **urinary system** includes two kidneys, two ureters, the bladder, and a urethra.

**Kidneys** are reddish-brown, bean shaped organs located at the back of the abdominal cavity between the spinal level of T10 and L3; on top of each kidney is an adrenal gland.

The **nephron** is the functional unit of the kidney; there are 2 to 3 million nephrons in the kidney; a nephron consists of a **Bowman's capsule**, **glomerulus**, and a **renal tubule**.

As the kidneys filter blood, they remove a certain amount of water and nitrogenous waste products of metabolism (**urea**, **uric acid**, **ammonia**, and some drugs).

The kidneys also function as endocrine glands, producing **erythropoietin**, a hormone released in response to lowered levels of oxygen in the blood, and **calcitriol (vitamin D3)**, the active form of vitamin D that stimulates the bone marrow to produce more red blood cells.

**Ureters**:

Two narrow tubes extending from the kidneys; each tube is about 12 inches long, 1/8 to ¼ inch in diameter.

**Peristalsis** moves urine down into the bladder.

As the bladder fills, it presses against the ureters, compressing them, and preventing a reverse flow of urine.

**Urinary bladder**:

The **bladder** is a muscular, hollow organ that lies in the pelvis and acts as a reservoir for urine.

When the bladder accumulates about a pint of urine, sensors indicate it is time to urinate.

Emptying the bladder is accomplished by a muscle called the **detrusor muscle**, a sphincter muscle at the mouth of the **urethra**.

**Urethra**: is the tube that carries urine from the bladder.

The male urethra is about 8 inches long and serves to pass urine and semen; the female urethra is about 1½ inches long, lies anterior to the vagina, and functions only to pass urine.

The opening at the end of the urethra is called the **meatus**; the close proximity of the female urethra to the anus allows bacteria to migrate up the urinary tract, predisposing females to urinary tract infections.

## Tissue Injury and Repair

There are two injury types: A **primary injury** is an injury from acute or chronic trauma. A **secondary injury** is an inflammatory response to a primary injury.

**Acute** and **chronic** are terms that describe a condition, pain, or illness.

**Acute** refers to a condition with a sudden onset and relatively short duration.

**Acute** pain is sharp; resulting from an incident or illness, but it is usually temporary.

**Chronic** refers to a lingering or ongoing condition.

**Chronic** pain is persistent or intermittent over a long period, often dull, spread over a large area, and many times without an identifiable source or cause.

A **chronic** illness progresses slowly, is difficult or impossible to remedy, and can last for weeks, months, years, or can be lifelong.

## Acute Soft Tissue Injury

A natural process of healing and repair takes place when soft tissue is injured, known as the **inflammatory response**.

**Inflammation** is a protective tissue response characterized by swelling, redness, heat, and pain.

Once tissue is injured, the process of healing begins immediately.

### The Healing Process

There are three phases of tissue healing: the Inflammatory response phase, the Fibroblastic repair phase, and the Maturation remodeling phase.

### Inflammatory phase:

When tissue is injured, histamines are released that cause blood vessels in the area of the damaged tissues to dilate, increasing blood flow to the area and causing redness and heat.

Capillary walls become more permeable, allowing large quantities of blood plasma and white blood cells to enter the tissue spaces, resulting in swelling. The swelling puts pressure on local nerve endings, causing pain. The initial effusion of blood and plasma lasts 24 to 36 hours.

*Leukocytes* and *phagocytes* (white blood cells) flood the area to engulf and digest (*phagocytosis*) the invading organisms and the damaged tissue debris. *Fibroblasts* (connective tissue cells) begin to lay down a random network of *fibrin* to secure the damaged tissue.

The *acute phase* lasts anywhere from a matter of *hours up to 72 hours* depending on the nature of the injury and the condition of the client. Massage and any treatment that might disrupt the delicate fibrin structures is *contraindicated*.

During this time, proper treatment includes (*PRICE*) protecting the area, rest, ice, compression and elevation. *PRICE* helps to reduce some of the swelling and pain is greatly reduced.

**Regenerative/Repair Phase:**

During the **repair phase** (*48 hours to six weeks*), increased fibroblast activity generate collagen fibers that randomly create bridges to bind tissues together. This creates an adhesion or scarring of the damaged tissue and creates a cross-linking between fascial sheaths.

The period of scar formation, referred to as *fibroplasia*, begins in the first few days after injury and *can last 4 to 6 weeks*.

The strength and stability of the tissue improves, but the cross-linking in the fascia and scarring can negatively affect functionality. It is essential to employ gentle techniques that encourage alignment of the collagen network to restore stability as well as function.

Techniques include mild lengthening with passive, pain-free range of motion and light cross-fiber manipulations. Non-weight bearing, active range of motion helps to restore mobility and produce strong, pliable scar tissue.

**Remodeling Phase:**

The remodeling phase of the healing process is a long-term process. During this phase, realignment or remodeling of the collagen fibers that make up scar tissue form a matrix in a position of maximum efficiency parallel to the lines of tension.

The tissue gradually assumes normal function and appearance. By week 3, a strong, contracted non vascular scar exists. The remodeling phase of healing may require several years to be complete.

**Wolff's law** states that bone and soft tissue will respond to the physical demands placed on them, causing them to remodel or realign along lines of tensile force.

After a brief period of immobilization during the inflammatory phase, the repair phase is an opportunity to return the tissue to normal flexibility and strength through controlled mobilization activity.

As the remodeling phase begins, incorporating aggressive range of motion and strengthening exercises are important to facilitate tissue remodeling and realignment. The amount of pain a client experiences will dictate the rate of progression.

### Factors That Delay Healing

**Atrophy:** Muscle wasting begins immediately with an injury. Early mobilization and strengthening of the injured area slows down atrophy.

**Age, Health, and Nutrition:** As we age, the elastic qualities of the skin decrease. Degenerative diseases, such as *arteriosclerosis* and *diabetes*, may hinder the healing process and become a concern for elderly clients.

Meeting the Dietary Recommended Intake (*DRI*) for vitamins is adequate for healing. Nutrients that are important: *amino acids* aid in the healing process, *zinc* is critical for enzyme systems, *vitamin A* for the immune system, *vitamin C* for collagen synthesis, and *vitamin K* for clotting.

**Corticosteroids:** The use of steroids in the early stages of the healing process has shown to inhibit capillary proliferation, collagen synthesis, fibroplasia, and increases in tensile strength of the healing scar tissue.

**Edema:** Swelling slows the healing process, causes tissue separation, inhibits neuromuscular control and slow nutrition to the injured area.

**Extent of tissue injury:** *Microtears* of soft tissue involve minor damage and is often associated with overuse. *Macrotears* of the soft tissue involves significant damage and are usually caused by acute trauma.

**Infection:** The presence of bacteria can impede the healing process.

**Hemorrhage:** Bleeding has the same negative effects on the healing process just as the buildup of edema.

**Poor Vascular Supply:** Injuries with limited or poor vascular supply heal slowly and poorly.

**Separation of Tissue:** If tissue is torn smooth and the edges are close together, it tends to heal with minimal scarring. If tissue is torn jagged with the edges separated, it will heal with *granulation tissue* (new vascular tissue) filling the spaces and have more scarring.

## Concepts of Energetic Anatomy

In East Asia, the whole of existence is thought to be intertwined with a vast web of invisible energy. India has named it **prana** and the cultures of Asia have named it **Qi** in China or **Ki** in Japan.

In the West, we have developed the term **orgone** or describe it as the vital life force in all living matter (**bioenergy**).

The first written descriptions of massage therapy are found in the oldest Chinese medical text, entitled *The Yellow Emperor's Classic of Internal Medicine* (**Huang Ti**).

Chinese ideograms depict a human being's connection with heaven and earth by portraying the human body with branches reaching into the sky from the tips of extended fingers and roots spreading from the feet grounded to earth.

"Blend the breath of heaven and the breath of earth with that of your own, becoming the breath of life itself (Morihei Ueshiba).

A comprehensive system of health and well-being known as **traditional Chinese medicine (TCM)** was created from the insights of the ancient sages of China.

**TCM** views everything in existence, all matter, is composed of a fundamental substance known as **Qi**. **Qi** is the vital force of the universe that infuses the human body and flows through it in a complex system of energy channels (**meridians**).

There are **twelve organ meridians** or channels that run bilaterally and are classified as being **yin** (solid) or **yang** (hollow). **Yin** and **Yang** is the concept that a polarity of forces exists throughout the universe, actively changing throughout the day, season, and lifetime to maintain an overall balance.

**Yin** is the feminine power of nurturing, soothing, and encompassing. It represents the shady side of a hill. **Yang** is the driving, masculine force of action and movement. It represents the sunny side of a hill. They both represent constant change and movement which is one of the central pillars of Chinese philosophy.

## The Twelve Organ Meridians

The human body has **six Yin organs** and **six Yang organs**. Each Yin organ is paired with a Yang organ by a special Yin/Yang relationship. Paired Yin and Yang organs belong to the same element in the **Five Element theory**. Their functions are closely related and disease in one usually affects the other.

**Lung** (Yin), Element (*Metal*), Location: ***Chest to end of thumb***; **Large Intestine** (Yang), Element (*Metal*), Location: ***Index finger to toe***

**Spleen** (Yin), Element (*Earth*), Location: ***Medial side of large toe to inside of leg to chest***; **Stomach** (Yang), Element (*Earth*), Location: ***Face to front of body to end of second toe***

**Heart** (Yin), Element (*Fire*), Location: ***Chest, near axilla to inside of arm to end of little finger***; **Small Intestine** (Yang), Element (*Fire)*, Location: ***Small finger to back of arm to side of face***

**Kidney** (Yin), Element (*Water*), Location: ***Bottom of foot and along inside of leg to upper chest***; **Bladder** (Yang), Element (*Water*), Location: ***Medial side of eye, over head, and down back and back of leg to little toe***

**Pericardium** (Yin), Element (*Fire*), Location: ***Chest to end of middle finger***; **Triple warmer** (Yang), Element (*Fire*), Location: ***End of ring finger back to side of head***

**Liver** (Yin), Element (*Wood*), Location: ***Big toe and along inside of leg to the bottom of the rib cage***; **Gallbladder** (Yang), Element (*Wood*), Location: ***Side of head and body and alongside leg to fourth toe***

**Two Extraordinary Vessels**, known as the *Conception vessel* (Yin) and the *Governing vessel* (Yang), are part of the **Eight Extra Meridians** which store and release energy to the twelve organ meridians as needed for regulation and harmonization of **Qi**.

**Conception vessel** (Yin), Location: ***Perineum and up the front of midline to bottom lip and chin***

**Governing vessel** (Yang), Location: ***Tip of tailbone, up midline of back, and over the head to upper lip***

The remaining extra meridians are the *Regulatory channel of yin*, the *Regulatory channel of yang*, the *Connecting channel of yin*, the *Connecting channel of yang*, the *belt channel*, and the *Vital or penetrating channel*.

These meridians have small areas of high conductivity called **acupoints** (acupuncture points). There are **365 acupoints**, located on the organ meridians where the **Qi** flows more superficially. **Pressure, heat, electricity, needles,** and **touch** can influence and affect the meridians.

### The Five Elements

Energy or **Qi** is broken down into five elements. The **Five Element theory** breaks down everything into five fundamental energies, substances, and qualities that constitute our existence: **wood, fire, earth, metal, and water**.

The **Ko** or **Control cycle: Wood** controls **earth** by covering or holding it in place with roots. **Earth** controls **water** by damming it or containing it. **Water** controls **fire** by extinguishing or dousing it. **Fire** controls **metal** by melting it. **Metal** controls **wood** by cutting it.

The **Shen** or **Creative cycle: Water** begets **wood**, **wood** fuels **fire**, **fire** creates **earth** (ashes), **earth** begets **metal**, and **metal** begets **water**.

## The Seven Chakras

The word **chakra** is derived from Sanskrit, the dominant classical language of the Indian subcontinent. **Chakra** means *disk* or *wheel*. There are **seven major chakras** or energy centers located between the base of the spine and the top of the head.

**Chakras** are considered to be rotating energy vortices with focal areas for reabsorption and transmission of energy. They include:

1. The **Root chakra** (Muladhara) is concerned with **survival** and **physical needs**. It represents our foundation and feeling of being grounded and is located in the tailbone area.

2. The **Sacral** or **Belly chakra** (Svadhisthana) is concerned with **emotional balance** and **sexuality**. It represents our connection and ability to accept others and new experiences. It is located in the lower abdomen about two inches below the navel.

3. The **Solar Plexus chakra** (Manipura) is concerned with **personal power** and **self-will**. It represents our ability to be confident and in control of our lives. It is located in the upper abdomen in the stomach area.

4. The **Heart chakra** (Anahata) is concerned with **love** and **relationships**. It represents our ability to love and is located at the center of the chest just above the heart.

5. The **Throat chakra** (Vishudda) is concerned with **communication** and **self-expression**. It represents our ability to communicate and is located in the throat.

6. The **Third eye** (Ajna) is concerned with **intuition** and **wisdom**. It represents our ability to focus on and see the big picture. It is located at the forehead between the eyes.

7. The **Crown chakra** is concerned with **spirituality**. It represents our ability to be fully connected spiritually and is located at the very top of the head.

### Methods of Energy Assessment and Treatment

One of the main assessment tools used in **TCM** is **pulse diagnosis**. According to TCM, an experienced practitioner can discern more than 25 varying qualities in pulses.

There are **three main pulse positions** taken at the radial artery, and each position has a **yang** (superficial) and **yin** (deep) location that accounts for all 12 major organs. Diagnosis of the tongue is usually paired with pulse diagnosis and they are the most frequently used forms of TCM assessment.

Another form of TCM assessment is known as the **Four Traditional Methods of Assessment** that includes listening, smelling, palpation, and looking.

There are various methods of treating energy. One of the oldest and widely practiced energetic modalities is **acupuncture** which dates back more than 5,000 years. **Acupuncture** uses very fine, sterile needles inserted into the superficial layer of the skin to stimulate specific **acupoints**. **Acupuncture** treatment is used to balance the energy system and assist the body in self-healing.

**Shiatsu**, which means **finger pressure**, uses the energy pathways on the meridians called **tsubos** to increase circulation of Qi and restore energy balances in the body.

**Tuina** is a vigorous form of bodywork that uses strong techniques to move energy along the meridians. Other forms of energy work include Marma-Point Therapy, Polarity Therapy, Reiki, Thai Massage, and Therapeutic Touch.

# Kinesiology (11%)

## Components and characteristics of muscles

Muscle is the main organ of the muscular system. Muscle movement is responsible for locomotion and all motor functions. Muscle comprises 40 to 60% of the total body weight and the skeletal muscular system consists of more than 600 muscles.

## Four Major Functions of Muscle

1. To produce movement

2. To stabilize joints

3. To maintain posture

4. To generate heat

### Types of Muscle:

**Skeletal (striated)** or **voluntary** muscles are controlled by conscious will.

**Smooth (visceral** or **involuntary)** muscles are controlled by the autonomic nervous system.

**Cardiac (heart)** muscle is only found in the heart. It is striated like skeletal muscle.

## Characteristics of Muscles

**Excitability** is the capacity of muscles to receive and react to stimuli.

**Contractility** is the ability of a muscle to contract or shorten and thereby exert force.

**Elasticity** refers to the tissue's ability to return to normal resting length when a stress that has been placed on it is removed.

**Extensibility** is the ability of a muscle to stretch.

## Concepts of muscle contractions

### Types of Muscle Contraction:

**Isometric contraction** – occurs when a muscle contracts and the ends of the muscle do not move.

**Isotonic contraction** – occurs when a muscle contracts and the distance between the ends of the muscle changes. Concentric contractions occur as the angle of the joint decreases. Eccentric contractions occur as the angle of joint increases.

## Excitability to Contractility to Elasticity

An electrical signal (**stimulus** or **action potential**) travels down a nerve cell causing it to release the neurotransmitter **acetylcholine** into the gap (**synapse**) between the nerve end and muscle fiber.

**Acetylcholine** crosses the gap, binds to a receptor on the muscle-cell membrane (**sarcolemma**) and causes an action potential in the muscle cell.

The action potential rapidly spreads along the muscle cell and enters the cell through the **transverse tubules**. **Transverse tubules** are a system of channels within the muscle cell containing extracellular fluid that helps transmit nerve impulses throughout the cell.

The action potential opens gates in the **sarcoplasmic reticulum**. The **Sarcoplasmic reticulum** is a network of membranous channels within the muscle cell that release calcium ions, causing muscle contractions.

**Calcium ions** flow into the **sarcomere**, the smallest functional unit of the muscle cell containing the **actin** (thin filament) and **myosin** (thick filament) filaments. **Myosin** is a protein that forms filaments that make up nearly 50% of muscle tissue and are involved in muscle contraction. **Actin** is a protein in muscle tissue that forms filaments that interact with myosin filaments to cause muscle contractions.

Calcium ions bind to **troponin** and **tropomyosin** molecules where cross-bridges from the **myosin** attach to active sites on the **actin** subunits of the filaments causing the muscle cell to shorten.

Sliding or contracting of these filaments continues as long as the calcium signal and ATP are present.

**Elasticity** or relaxation occurs when the nerve impulse no longer stimulates calcium release and the **myosin** can no longer grip the **actin**, and the sliding reverses.

# Proprioceptors

**Proprioception** is a system of sensory and motor nerve activity that provides information to the CNS about the position and rate of movement of different body parts.

**Proprioceptors** are specialized nerve endings located in muscle, tendons, joints, or fascia. They sense where the body is and how it moves.

**Kinesthesia** is the unconscious inner sense of position and movement of the body.

## Proprioceptors are of three major categories

**Muscle spindle cells** – located largely in the belly of the muscle, are sensory organs in muscle that detect the rate of stretch in muscles.

**Golgi tendon organs** – located in tendons, are multibranched sensory nerve endings that measure the amount of tension produced in muscle cells as a result of the muscles' stretching and contracting.

**Joint Proprioceptors** – located in the connective tissue or fascia surrounding the joints, are mechanoreceptors of two types (Pacini's corpuscles and Ruffini's endings) that sense the position and movements of the joints.

## Locations, attachments (origins, insertions), actions and fiber directions of muscles

**Origin of a muscle** - is the point where the end of a muscle is anchored to an immovable section of the skeleton.

**Insertion of a muscle** - is the more mobile attachment of a muscle to bone.

**Agonist** – prime mover.

**Antagonist** – the muscle that performs the opposite movement of the agonist.

**Synergists** - muscles that assist the agonist.

**Fixator** – muscles that act to stabilize a body part so that another muscle can act on an adjacent limb or body part.

## Muscles of Mastication

**Masseter – Origin**: Zygomatic arch; **Insertion**: Angle and ramus of mandible; Action: elevate the mandible (temporomandibular joint), may assist to protract the mandible (TM joint)

**Temporalis – Origin**: Temporal fossa and fascia; **Insertion**: Coronoid process and anterior edge of ramus of mandible; Action: elevate the mandible; retract the mandible

## Muscles of the Neck

<u>**Anterior triangle of the neck**</u>:

**Suprahyoid muscles** – Affect movement of the tongue; elevate the hyoid bone; help produce sound and speech; draw the larynx and thyroid cartilage downward; depress the larynx; and elevate thyroid cartilage.

**Infrahyoid muscles** – Depress the hyoid bone; influence swallowing; help produce sound.

**Posterior triangle of the neck**:

**Longus colli** and **capitus** – bend the neck forward (flexion); oblique portion bends neck laterally; inferior portion rotates neck to the opposite side; control elevation of cervical extension; lateral extension and contralateral rotation; and provide dynamic stabilization of cervical spine.

**Scalene group**:

**Scalenus anterior** – bends the cervical portion of the vertebral column forward and laterally; also rotates to the opposite side and assists in elevation of the first rib, thus functioning as an accessory muscle of respiration; decelerates cervical lateral flexion and rotation; and stabilizes cervical spine.

**Scalenus medius** – acting from above, helps to raise the first rib, thus functioning as an accessory muscle of respiration; acting from below, bends the cervical part of the vertebral column to the same side; assists flexion of the neck; decelerates cervical lateral flexion and rotation; and stabilizes cervical spine.

**Scalenus posterior** – bends the lower end of the cervical portion of the vertebral column to the same side (lateral flexion); helps to elevate the second rib, thus functioning as an accessory muscle of respiration; decelerates cervical lateral flexion and rotation; and stabilizes cervical spine.

**Sternocleidomastoid** – assists in flexing the cervical portion of the vertebral column forward, elevating thorax, and extending the head at the atlantooccipital joint; stabilizes the head; resists forceful backward movement of the head, tilts head, rotates the head, and simultaneously acts to control rotation.

**Deep posterior cervical muscles**:

**Splenius capitus** and **cervicis** – extend head and neck, draw head dorsally and laterally and rotate head to the same side; check and control cervical flexion and contralateral rotation; stabilize cervical spine.

## Erector Spinae Group

**Spinalis thoracis, cervicis**, and **capitis**; **Longissimus thoracis, cervicis**, and **capitis**; **Iliocostalis lumborum, thoracis**, and **cervicis** – extend, rotate, and laterally flex the vertebral column and head; assist with anterior tilt elevation and rotation of the pelvis and spinal stabilization; control and decelerate vertebral flexor rotation and lateral flexion; stabilize lumbar spine primarily.

## Gluteal Group

**Gluteus maximus** – **Origin**: Coccyx edge of sacrum, posterior iliac crest, sacrotuberous and the sacroiliac ligaments; **Insertion**: Iliotibial tract of Fascia lata & gluteal tuberosity of femur; **Action**:

Extends & laterally rotates thigh, support extended knee; **Major antagonists**: Iliopsoas, tensor fasciae latae, and gluteus medius (anterior fibers)

**Gluteus medius** – **Origin**: Gluteal surface of ilium, between posterior & anterior gluteal lines, just below iliac crest; **Insertion**: Greater trochanter of femur; **Action**: Abduction & medial rotation at hip; **Major antagonists**: adductors of the thigh

**Gluteus minimus** – **Origin**: Gluteal surface of the ilium between the anterior and inferior gluteal lines; **Insertion**: Anterior aspect of greater trochanter; **Action**: abduct, medially rotate and flex the hip; **Major antagonists**: adductors of the thigh

**Tensor fasciae latae** – **Origin**: Iliac crest, posterior to ASIS; **Insertion**: Iliotibial tract; **Action**: abduct, medially rotate and flex the hip; **Major antagonists**: Gluteus medius (posterior fibers), adductors of the thigh, gluteus maximus, and hamstrings

### Adductor Group: Medial Thigh Muscles

**Major Antagonists**: Gluteus medius, Gluteus minimus, tensor fasciae latae, and hamstrings

**Adductor brevis** – **Origin**: Inferior ramus of pubis; **Insertion**: Pectineal line and medial lip of linea aspera; **Action**: adduction, flexion, and medial rotation at the hip

**Adductor longus** – **Origin**: Inferior ramus of pubis, anterior to adductor brevis; **Insertion**: Linea aspera of femur; **Action**: adduction, flexion, and medial rotation at the hip

**Adductor magnus** – **Origin**: Inferior ramus of pubis, posterior to adductor brevis and ischial tuberosity; **Insertion**: Linea aspera and adductor tubercle of femur; **Action**: (whole) adduction at hip, (Anterior) flexion & medial rotation, (Posterior) extension & lateral rotation; **Major Antagonists**: (same as above) omit hamstrings, add iliopsoas

**Gracilis** – **Origin**: Inferior ramus of pubis; **Insertion**: Proximal, medial shaft of tibia at pes anserinus tendon; **Action**: adduction and medial rotation at hip; flex and medially rotate the knee

**Pectineus** – **Origin**: Superior ramus of pubis; **Insertion**: Pectineal line of femur; **Action**: adduction, flexion, and medial rotation at the hip

### Lateral Rotators of the Hip

**Major antagonists**: Anterior fibers of the gluteus medius, gluteus minimus, and the tensor fasciae latae

**Piriformis** – **Origin**: Anterior surface of sacrum; **Insertion**: Superior aspect of greater trochanter; **Action**: laterally rotate the hip; abduct the hip when the hip is flexed

**Quadratus Femoris** – **Origin**: Lateral border of ischial tuberosity; **Insertion**: Intertrochanteric crest, between the greater and lesser trochanters; **Action**: laterally rotate the hip

**Obturator Internus** – **Origin**: Obturator membrane and inferior surface of obturator foramen; **Insertion**: Medial surface of greater trochanter; **Action**: laterally rotate the hip

**Obturator Externus** – **Origin**: Rami of pubis and ischium, obturator membrane; **Insertion**: Trochanteric fossa of femur; **Action**: laterally rotate the hip

**Gemellus Superior** – **Origin**: Ischial spine; **Insertion**: Medial surface of greater trochanter; **Action**: laterally rotate the hip

**Gemellus Inferior** – **Origin**: Ischial tuberosity; **Insertion**: Medial surface of greater trochanter; **Action**: laterally rotate the hip

## Iliopsoas

**Iliacus** – **Origin**: Iliac fossa; **Insertion**: Femur distal to lesser trochanter of femur; **Action**: Flexion at hip (see above image)

**Psoas major** – **Origin**: Bodies and transverse processes of lumbar vertebrae; **Insertion**: Lesser trochanter; **Action**: with **origin** fixed, flex the hip; with the **insertion** fixed, flex the trunk toward the thigh, tilt pelvis anteriorly; unilaterally, assist to laterally flex the lumbar spine

### Flexors of the knee

**Major Antagonist**: Quadricep femoris group, iliopsoas, tensor fasciae latae

**Biceps Femoris** – **Origin**: (Long head) Ischial tuberosity, (Short head) Lateral lip of linea aspera; **Insertion**: Head of fibula; **Action**: flex and laterally rotate knee, extend and laterally rotate hip, tilt pelvis posteriorly

**Semimembranosus** – **Origin**: Ischial tuberosity; **Insertion**: Posterior aspect of medial condyle of tibia; **Action**: flex and medially rotate knee, extend and medially rotate hip, tilt pelvis posteriorly

**Semitendinosus** - **Origin**: Ischial tuberosity; **Insertion**: Proximal, medial shaft of tibia at pes anserinus tendon; **Action**: flex and medially rotate knee, extend and medially rotate hip, tilt pelvis posteriorly

**Sartorius** - **Origin**: Anterior superior iliac spine (ASIS); **Insertion**: Proximal, medial shaft of tibia at pes anserinus tendon; **Action**: flex, laterally rotate and abduct hip, flex and medially rotate knee **Major Antagonist**: Quadricep femoris group, Hamstrings, tensor fasciae latae, adductor group of thigh

**Popliteus - Origin**: Lateral condyle of the femur; **Insertion**: Proximal, posterior aspect of tibia; **Action**: flex and medially rotate knee; **Major Antagonist**: Quadricep femoris group, biceps femoris

## Extensors of the knee

**Major Antagonist**: Hamstrings for all; plus gluteus maximus for Rectus femoris

**Rectus Femoris - Origin**: Anterior inferior iliac spine (AIIS); **Insertion**: Tibial tuberosity; **Action**: extend knee, flex hip

**Vastus intermedius – Origin**: Anterior and lateral shaft of femur; **Insertion**: Tibial tuberosity; **Action**: extend knee

**Vastus lateralis - Origin**: Lateral lip of linea aspera, gluteal tuberosity and greater trochanter; **Insertion**: Tibial tuberosity; **Action**: extend knee

**Vastus medialis - Origin**: Medial lip of linea aspera; **Insertion**: Tibial tuberosity; **Action**: extend knee

## Action at the ankle

**Dorsiflexors – Major antagonists**: Gastrocnemius, Soleus, Tibialis posterior, Peroneus (Fibularis) longus and brevis (assists)

**Tibialis anterior – Origin**: Lateral condyle of tibia; proximal, lateral surface of tibia and interosseous membrane; **Insertion**: Medial cuneiform and base of first metatarsal; **Action**: Invert foot, Dorsiflex ankle

**Extensor digitorum longus - Origin**: Lateral condyle of tibia; proximal, anterior shaft of fibula and interosseous membrane; **Insertion**: Middle and distal phalanges of second-fifth toes; **Action**: Extend second-fifth toes, Dorsiflex ankle, and Evert foot

**Extensor hallucis longus - Origin**: Middle, anterior surface of fibula and interosseous membrane; **Insertion**: Distal phalanx of first toe; **Action**: Extend first toe, Dorsiflex ankle and Invert foot

## Plantar flexors

**Gastrocnemius – Origin**: Condyles of femur, posterior surfaces; **Insertion**: Calcaneus via calcaneal tendon; **Action**: flex knee and plantar flex ankle; **Major antagonists**: Tibialis anterior, extensor digitorum/hallucis longus, and quadriceps femoris group

**Soleus – Origin**: Soleal line; proximal, posterior surface of tibia and posterior aspect of head of fibula; **Insertion**: Calcaneus via calcaneal tendon; **Action**: plantar flex ankle; **Major antagonists**: Tibialis anterior, and extensor digitorum/hallucis longus

**Plantaris - Origin**: Lateral supracondylar line of femur; **Insertion**: Calcaneus via calcaneal tendon; **Action**: Plantar flex ankle (weak) and flex knee (weak); **Major antagonists**: Tibialis anterior and quadriceps femoris group

**Fibularis (peroneus) brevis - Origin**: Distal two-thirds of lateral fibula; **Insertion**: Tuberosity of fifth metatarsal; **Action**: Evert foot and plantar flex ankle (assist); **Major antagonists**: Tibialis anterior

**Fibularis (peroneus) longus – Origin**: Head of fibula and proximal two-thirds of lateral fibula; **Insertion**: Base of first metatarsal and medial cuneiform; **Action**: Evert foot and plantar flex ankle (assist); **Major antagonists**: Tibialis anterior

**Tibialis posterior – Origin**: Proximal, posterior shafts of tibia and fibula; and interosseous membrane; **Insertion**: All five tarsal bones and bases of second-fourth metatarsals; **Action**: Invert foot, plantar flex ankle; **Major antagonists**: Tibialis anterior, Peroneus (Fibularis) longus, Peroneus (Fibularis) brevis

### Action at the Toes

### <u>Digital Flexors</u>

**Flexor digitorum longus – Origin**: Middle, posterior surface of tibia; **Insertion**: Distal phalanges of second-fifth toes; **Action**: Flex second – fifth toes, invert foot, (weak) plantar flexion; **Major antagonists**: Extensor digitorum longus/brevis

**Flexor hallucis longus – Origin**: Middle half of posterior fibula; **Insertion**: Distal phalanx of first toe; **Action**: Flex first toe, invert foot, (weak) plantar flexion; **Major antagonists**: Extensor hallucis longus/brevis

### <u>Digital Extensors</u>

**Extensor digitorum longus - Origin**: Lateral condyle of tibia; proximal, anterior shaft of fibula and interosseous membrane; **Insertion**: Middle and distal phalanges of second – fifth toes; **Action**: Extend second-fifth toes, Dorsiflex ankle and Evert foot

**Extensor hallucis longus – Origin**: Middle, anterior surface of fibula and interosseous membrane; **Insertion**: Distal phalanx of first toe; **Action**: Extend first toe, Dorsiflex ankle, Invert foot

### Elbow Flexors

**Biceps Brachii – Origin**: (short head) coracoids process of scapula, (long head) tubercle at top of glenoid fossa of scapula; **Insertion**: posterior portion of radial tuberosity; **Action**: flexion of arm at elbow and shoulder supinates forearm; **Major Antagonists**: Triceps brachii, Pronator teres, Pronator quadratus, and posterior deltoid

**Brachialis – Origin**: Distal half of anterior aspect of humerus; **Insertion**: tuberosity of ulna; **Action**: Flexion of the elbow; **Major Antagonists**: Triceps brachii

**Brachioradialis – Origin**: Lateral supracondylar ridge of humerus; **Insertion**: Styloid process of radius; **Action**: Flexion of the elbow; **Major Antagonists**: Triceps brachii, Supinator, Pronator teres, and Pronator quadratus

### Elbow Extensors

**Anconeus – Origin**: Lateral epicondyle of humerus; **Insertion**: Olecranon process and posterior, proximal surface of ulna; **Action**: Extend elbow; **Major Antagonists**: Biceps brachii and brachialis

**Triceps Brachii – Origin**: (Long Head) Infraglenoid tubercle of scapula; (lateral Head) Posterior surface of proximal half of humerus; (Medial Head) Posterior surface of distal half of humerus; **Insertion**: Olecranon process of ulna; **Action**: (all heads) Extend elbow; (Long head) Extend shoulder, Adduct shoulder; **Major Antagonists**: Biceps brachii and brachialis

### Muscles That Move the Arm & Shoulder

**Latissimus Dorsi – Origin**: Inferior angle of scapula, spinous processes of last six thoracic vertebrae, last 3 or 4 ribs, thoracolumbar aponeurosis and posterior iliac crest; **Insertion**: Intertubercular groove of the humerus; **Action**: extend, adduct, and medially rotate the shoulder; **Major antagonists**: Clavicular head of the pectoralis major, teres minor, infraspinatus, deltoid, supraspinatus, levator scapulae and rectus abdominis

**Teres Major – Origin**: Inferior angle and lower one-third of lateral border of the scapula; **Insertion**: Crest of the lesser tubercle of the humerus; **Action**: extend, adduct, and medially rotate the shoulder; **Major antagonists**: teres minor, infraspinatus, anterior deltoid, supraspinatus, and pectoralis minor

**Coracobrachialis – Origin**: Coracoid process; **Insertion**: Medial margin of shaft of humerus; **Action**: Adduction & flexion at shoulder; **Major antagonist**: posterior deltoid

**Deltoid – (Anterior) Origin**: Lateral 1/3 of clavicle; **Insertion**: deltoid tuberosity of humerus; **Action**: Flexion, horizontal rotation; **(Middle) Origin**: Acromion & lateral spine of scapula; **Insertion**: Deltoid tuberosity of humerus; **Action**: Abduction to 90 degrees; **(Posterior) Origin**: Lower lip of the spine of scapula; **Insertion**: Deltoid tuberosity of humerus; **Action**: Extension, horizontal abduction, lateral rotation; **Major antagonists**: pectoralis major and latissimus dorsi; anterior and posterior deltoids are antagonistic to each other

## Rotator Cuff Muscles

**Supraspinatus – Origin**: Supraspinous fossa of scapula; **Insertion**: Greater tubercle of humerus; **Action**: Abduct shoulder and stabilize head of humerus in glenoid cavity

**Infraspinatus – Origin**: Infraspinous fossa of scapula; **Insertion**: Greater tubercle of humerus; **Action**: laterally rotate shoulder, stabilize head of humerus in glenoid cavity, and adduct shoulder

**Teres Minor – Origin**: Upper two-thirds of lateral border of scapula; **Insertion**: Greater tubercle of humerus; **Action**: laterally rotate shoulder, stabilize head of humerus in glenoid cavity, and adduct shoulder

**Subscapularis – Origin**: Subscapular fossa of scapula **Insertion**: Lesser tubercle of humerus; **Action**: medially rotate shoulder and stabilize head of humerus in glenoid cavity

## Muscles That Position the Pectoral Girdle

**Levator scapulae – Origin**: Transverse process of first-fourth cervical vertebrae; **Insertion**: Medial border of scapula, between superior angle and superior portion of spine of scapula; **Action**: elevate the scapula, downwardly rotate the scapula, laterally flex the neck, rotate the head and neck same side; bilaterally extend the head and neck

**Pectoralis minor – Origin**: Third, fourth and fifth ribs; **Insertion**: Medial surface of coracoid process of the scapula; **Action**: depress the scapula, abduct the scapula, downwardly rotate the scapula; with the scapula fixed, assists to elevate the thorax during forced inhalation

**Rhomboid major & minor – Origin**: Major- Spinous processes of T2 to T5; Minor- Spinous processes of C7 and T1; **Insertion**: Major- Medial border of the scapula between the spine of the scapula and inferior angle; Minor- Upper portion of medial border of the scapula, across from spine of scapula; **Action**: adduct, elevate and downwardly rotate the scapula

**Serratus anterior – Origin**: External surfaces of upper eight or nine ribs; **Insertion**: Anterior surface of medial border of the scapula; **Action**: abduct, upwardly rotate and depress the scapula; hold the medial border of scapula against the rib cage; with the scapula fixed, may act to elevate the thorax during forced inhalation

**Subclavis** – **Origin**: First rib and cartilage; **Insertion**: Inferior surface of middle one-third of clavicle; **Action**: depress the clavicle and draw it anteriorly; elevate the first rib; stabilize the sternoclavicular joint

**Trapezius** – **Origin**: External occipital protuberance, medial portion of superior nuchal line of the occiput, ligamentum nuchae and spinous processes of C7-T12; **Insertion**: Lateral one-third of clavicle, Acromion and spine of the scapula; **Action**: **Bilaterally**- Extend the head and neck; **Unilaterally**- laterally flex the head and neck to the same side, rotate the head and neck to the opposite side, elevate and upwardly rotate the scapula; **Middle fibers**- Adduct and stabilize the scapula; **Lower fibers**- Depress and upwardly rotate the scapula

**Diaphragm** – **Origin**: Xiphoid process, ribs 7-12 & anterior surfaces of lumbar vertebrae; **Insertion**: Central tendinous sheet; **Action**: Main muscle of respiration, contraction expands thoracic cavity, compresses abdominopelvic cavity

**External Intercostals** – **Origin**: Inferior border of each rib; **Insertion**: Superior border of more inferior rib; **Action**: Elevates ribs

**Internal intercostals** – **Origin**: Superior border of each rib; **Insertion**: Inferior border of the more superior rib; **Action**: Depresses ribs

**External Oblique** – **Origin**: Ribs 5-12; **Insertion**: Extend to linea alba & iliac crest; **Action**: Compresses abdomen, depresses ribs, laterally flexes or rotates vertebral column

**Internal Oblique** – **Origin**: Inguinal ligament, thoracolumbar fascia & iliac crest; **Insertion**: Inferior surfaces of ribs 9-12, costal cartilages 8-10, linea alba & pubis; **Action**: Compresses abdomen, depresses ribs, laterally flexes or rotates vertebral column

**Flexor Carpi Radialis** – **Origin**: Medial epicondyle of humerus; **Insertion**: Bases of 2nd & 3rd metacarpal bones; **Action**: Flexion & abduction at wrist

**Pronator Teres**- **Origin**: Medial epicondyle of humerus & coronoid process of ulna; **Insertion**: Middle of lateral surface of radius; **Action**: Pronates forearm and hand by medial rotation of radius at radioulnar joints & flexion at elbow

## Joint structure and function

**Joints** or **Articulations** – are places where bones come together, where limbs are attached and where the motion of the skeletal system occurs.

**Types of Joints**: Classified according to the amount of motion they permit.

**Synarthrotic joints** – are essentially immovable; such as those in the skull.

**Amphiarthrotic joints** – have limited motion; such as the symphysis pubis and sacroiliac joints.

**Diarthrotic joints** – are freely movable and are capable of several kinds of movements:

**Joint Structure**: Immovable joints (**Synarthrotic**) and slightly movable joints (**Amphiarthrotic**) are fibrous or cartilaginous joints. Freely movable joints (**Diarthrotic**) are synovial joints. **Synovial joints** are freely movable joints with a joint cavity surrounded by an articular capsule.

### Types of Movable Joints

*Classification of Diarthrotic/Synovial Joints by Movements*: Three main categories are **uniaxial**, **biaxial**, and **multiaxial**.

A **Uniaxial joint** is constructed so that visible motion of the bony components is allowed in only one of the planes of the body around a single axis (pivot and hinge joints).

A *Pivot joint* has an extension on one bone that rotates in relation to the bone it articulates with; the atlas and axis bones of the neck or the proximal ends of the radius and ulna just distal to the elbow.

A *Hinge joint* allows flexion and extension; move through one plane only; elbow, knee, and two distal joints of the fingers.

**Multiiaxial joints** are joints in which the bony components are free to move in three planes (**triaxial**) around the axes (**ball-and-socket** and **gliding joints**).

*Ball-and-socket joints* movements allowed are flexion, extension, abduction, adduction, rotation, and circumduction; permit the greatest range of movement; hips and shoulders.

*Gliding joints* have nearly flat surfaces that permit gliding between two or more bones; the spine or carpal and tarsal.

**Biaxial joints** allow movement in two planes around two axes; allow flexion, extension, abduction, adduction (saddle and condyloid joints).

*Saddle joints* involve bones with concave articulating surfaces; thumb, sternoclavicular joint and ankle joint.

*Condyloid* or *Ellipsoid joints* have an oval-shaped end of one bone that articulates with an ellipsoid basin of another; between the distal end of the radius and trapezium at the wrist.

## Movements of Joints

The standard anatomic body position is defined as standing erect with the head, toes, and palms of the hands facing forward with the fingers extended.

**Cardinal Planes of the Body**: *Frontal plane*, *Sagittal plane*, and *Transverse plane*

**Coronal/Frontal plane** divides the body into front and back parts; movements in this plane are abduction and adduction.

**Sagittal plane** divides the body into right and left sides; movements in this plane are flexion and extension.

**Transverse/Horizontal plane** divides the body into upper and lower parts; rotations occur in this plane; external and internal rotation.

## General Joint Movements

**Flexion**: bending movement that decreases the angle of a joint by bringing bones together.

**Extension**: straightening movement that increases the angle of a joint by moving bones apart.

**Abduction**: lateral movement away from the midline of the trunk.

**Diagonal abduction**: movement of a limb through a diagonal plane directly across and away from the midline of the body; ex. moving the right arm from in front of the left hip to in front of the right shoulder.

**Horizontal abduction**: movement of the humerus in the horizontal plane away from the midline of the body.

**Adduction**: movement medially toward the midline of the trunk.

**Diagonal adduction**: movement by a limb through a diagonal plane toward and across the midline of the body; ex. return of the right arm from a flexed position to in front of the left hip.

**Horizontal adduction**: movement of the humerus in the horizontal plane toward the midline of the body.

**Circumduction**: circular movement of a limb, combining the movements of flexion, extension, abduction, and adduction, to create a cone shape; ex. doing arm circles.

**Rotation**: twisting or turning of a bone on its own axis; ex. turning the head from side to side.

**Internal rotation**: rotation medially toward the midline of the body.

**External rotation**: rotation laterally away from the midline of the body.

### Specific Joint Movements of the Forearm, Thumb, Ankle, and Wrist

**Pronation**: internal rotation of the radius where it lies diagonally across the ulna; palm-down position of the forearm.

**Supination**: external rotation of the radius where it lies parallel to the ulna; palms-up position of the forearm.

**Opposition of the thumb**: diagonal movement of the thumb across the palmer surface of the hand to make contact with the fingers.

**Eversion**: turning the sole of the foot outward.

**Inversion**: turning of the sole of the foot inward or medially.

**Dorsiflexion**: flexion movement of the ankle resulting in the top of the foot moving toward the anterior tibia bone; ex. walking on the heels.

**Plantar flexion**: extension movement of the ankle that results in the foot or toes moving away from the body; ex. pressing the gas pedal of an automobile.

**Radial flexion**: abduction movement at the wrist of the thumb side of the hand toward the forearm.

**Ulnar flexion**: adduction movement at the wrist of the little finger side of the hand toward the forearm.

### Specific Joint Movements of the Shoulder Girdle and Shoulder Joint

**Elevation**: movement of the shoulder girdle to become closer to the ears; ex. shrugging the shoulders.

**Depression**: inferior movement of the shoulder girdle; ex. returning to the normal position from a shoulder shrug.

**Protraction**: forward movement of the shoulder girdle away from the spine; ex. abduction of scapula.

**Retraction**: backward movement of the shoulder girdle toward the spine; ex. adduction of scapula.

**Rotary upward**: rotary movement of the scapula with the inferior angle of the scapula moving laterally and upward.

**Rotary downward**: rotary movement of the scapula with the inferior angle of the scapula moving medially and downward.

## Specific Joint Movements of the Spine and Pelvis

**Lateral flexion (side bending)**: movement of the head or trunk laterally away from the midline.

**Reduction**: return of the spinal column to the anatomic position from lateral flexion.

## Range of Motion/ROM

**Range of motion** is the action of a joint through the entire extent of its movement.

**Active (ROM)** – movements in which the client actively participates by contracting the muscles involved in the movement without practitioner intervention.

**Passive (ROM)** – movements in which the client remains relaxed and allows the practitioner to stretch the fibrous tissue and move the joint through its range of motion.

**Resistive (ROM)** – movement made by the client that is in some way resisted by the practitioner; used to test or improve mobility, flexibility, or strength depending on how the technique is performed.

# Pathology, Contraindications, Areas of Caution, Special Populations (13%)

## Overview of Pathologies

**Pathology** is the study of the structural and functional changes caused by disease; pathology occurs when homeostatic and restorative body mechanisms break down and can no longer adapt.

**Pathogen** – any virus, microorganism, or substance causing disease.

## Causes of Disease

### Pathogenic organisms and infectious agents:

**Prions** – pathogen composed of proteins that contain neither DNA nor RNA; begin as slightly malformed proteins in neurons that affect normal neuronal activity; causative agents for bovine spongiform encephalopathy (mad cow).

**Virus** – packets of DNA or RNA wrapped in a protein coat called a capsid; ***need a host to replicate***; infected cells eventually release copies of the virus called virions; two viruses of particular concern for health care professionals: Hepatitis B & C and herpes simplex.

**Bacteria** – single celled microorganisms that ***can survive outside of a host***; not all are pathogenic; others can cause serious illness (by invading healthy tissues or by releasing enzymes or toxins).

**Fungi** – a group of organisms that includes **yeast** and **molds**; most internal fungal infections are indications of imbalances that allow normal yeasts to replicate uncontrollably (candidiasis); ringworm, athlete's foot and jock itch are superficial fungal infections.

### Three animal parasites:

*Protozoa* – single-celled organisms cause diseases that include giardiasis, cryptosporidiosis (transmitted thru oral-fecal contamination) and malaria (vector borne).

*Helminths* & *roundworms* – parasitic worms colonize various places in the body (**GI tract**, liver, & urinary bladder); roundworms are common in the U.S. and the world (most prevalent in warm climates); schistosmiasis (can cause bladder cancer) and trichinosis are worm-related diseases.

*Anthropods* – head lice, crab lice, and the mites that cause scabies are animal parasites that colonize human skin.

***Others*** – mosquitoes (malaria, West Nile virus), ticks (Lyme disease, Rocky Mountain spotted fever), and fleas (bubonic plague) are common disease vectors.

**Genetic predisposition**: altered or mutated genes can cause abnormality; genetic disease is caused by genetic abnormality.

**Physical** or **chemical agents**: toxic or destructive chemicals, extreme heat and cold, mechanical injury, radiation, and metabolic agents such as alcohol, cigarettes, and drugs can affect the normal homeostasis of the body.

**Malnutrition**: insufficient or imbalanced intake of nutrients can cause a variety of diseases.

**Degeneration**: tissues sometimes break apart or degenerate; degeneration is a normal consequence of aging.

**Autoimmunity**: some diseases result from the immune system attacking the body and from mistakes or overreactions of the immune response; steroids are often used to treat autoimmune disease.

**Immune deficiency**: some diseases are caused by the failure of the immune system to defend against pathogens (cancer, HIV, AIDS).

**Tumors** and **cancer**: abnormal tissue growths from uncontrolled cell division called hyperplasia results in a neoplasm or tumor; the tumor is named from the tissue type – osteosarcoma is cancer of the bone; cells in the lymphatic system, epidermis, bone marrow, and **GI tract** are more prone to develop cancer cells.

## Development of Pathology

**Illness**: Illness occurs when a body process breaks down; illness tends to indicate general cautions and contraindications.

**Injury**: Injury occurs when tissue is damaged; injury more often creates regional cautions and contraindications.

**Signs**: are objective abnormalities that can be seen or measured by someone other than the patient.

**Symptoms**: are the subjective abnormalities felt only by the patient.

**Syndrome**: a syndrome is a group of different signs and symptoms, usually from a common cause.

**Acute**: a disease is classified as acute when signs and symptoms develop quickly, last a short time, and then disappear.

...eases that develop slowly and last for a long time (sometimes for life) are called chronic

...able diseases: can be transmitted from one person to the other.

...s: is the relative constancy of the body's internal environment; if homeostasis is disturbed, a disease process, a variety of feedback mechanisms usually attempt to return the body to

...rs: Certain predisposing conditions may make a disease more likely to develop.

**Genetic factors**: an inherited trait can put a person at a greater than normal risk, or predisposition, for a specific disease; changes in diet and lifestyle can support the body against the genetic tendency toward the disease process.

**Age**: biologic and behavioral factors increase the risk for certain diseases to develop at certain times in life; musculoskeletal problems are common between the ages of 30 and 50.

**Lifestyle**: the way we live and work can put us at risk for some diseases; smoking, excessive alcohol use, lack of exercise, poor nutrition, and poor sleep habits are examples of negative lifestyles.

**Stress**: stress may be defined as any substantial change in your routine or any activity that causes the body to adapt.

**Environment**: some environmental situations put us at greater risk for getting certain diseases; living in an area of high concentrations of pollution can increase the risk of respiratory problems.

**Preexisting conditions**: a preexisting condition can put a person at risk of a secondary condition; a viral infection can lead to a bacterial infection.

# Contraindications

## Cardiovascular System

**Anemia** - is a symptom rather than a disease in itself; it indicates a shortage of red blood cells (**RBCs**), **hemoglobin**, or both; Massage is: **indicated**.

**Aneurysm** – is a bulge in a vein, an artery, or the heart; they usually occur in the **thoracic** or **abdominal aorta** or in the arteries at the base of the brain; Massage is: **absolute contraindication**.

**Angina Pectoris** – a condition marked by severe pain in the chest; Massage is: **indicated**.

**Arteriosclerosis** – is the hardening of the arteries from any cause: Massage is: **absolute contraindication**.

**Atherosclerosis** – is a condition in which arteries become inelastic and brittle as a result of the deposit of plaques: Massage is: **absolute contraindication**.

**Embolism/Thrombus** – an **embolism** is a traveling clot or a collection of debris and a **thrombus** is a lodged clot; Massage is: **absolute contraindication**.

**Endocarditis** – is inflammation of the **endocardium**, especially where it covers the valves of the heart; Massage is: **absolute contraindication**.

**Hypertension** – is a technical term for **high blood pressure**; it is defined as blood pressure persistently elevated above **140 mm Hg systolic** and/ or **90 mm Hg diastolic**; Massage is: **indicated**.

**Heart attack (Myocardial infarction)** – is damage to the **myocardium** caused by an obstruction in blood flow through the coronary arteries, which results in permanent **myocardial** damage; Massage is: **conditionally indicated/ physician approval**.

**Hemophilia** – is a genetic disorder in which certain clotting factors in the blood are either insufficient or missing altogether; Massage is: **conditionally indicated/ physician approval**.

**Pericarditis** – is inflammation of the **pericardial sac**, but it may penetrate to the **myocardial** cells as well; it is usually due to a viral or bacterial infection; Massage is: **absolute contraindication**.

**Phlebitis** – inflammation of a vein, caused by trauma, pregnancy, prolonged periods of sitting or standing and may present blood clots; Massage is: **regional/local contraindication**.

**Raynaud's Syndrome** – is a condition defined by episodes of vasospasm followed by dilation of the arterioles, usually in fingers and toes, and occasionally in the nose, ears, and lips; Massage is: **indicated**.

**Transient Ischemic Attack (TIA)** – also called a "**mini-stroke**", occurs when the blockage is due to a small clot that melts within a few hours; damage may be mild, but cumulative; Massage is: **conditionally indicated/ physician approval**.

**Varicose Veins** – are distended veins, usually in the legs, caused by venous insufficiency and retrograde blood flow; Massage is: **regional/local contraindicated**.

### Digestive System

**Celiac Disease** is a digestive disease that damages the lining of the small intestine and prevents the absorption of nutrients. If a person with **celiac disease** eats foods containing **gluten** (a protein in wheat, rye and barley), their immune system responds by flattening or destroying the **villi** that help with the absorption of nutrients. Massage is: **indicated**; however, the characteristic skin rash that many celiac disease patients have **locally contraindicates** massage.

**Cholecystitis** is inflammation of the gallbladder from a stuck stone ("**lith**") or other cause; Massage is: **absolute contraindication**.

**Cirrhosis** means "**yellow condition**", referring to **jaundice** that can develop; is a condition in which normal liver cells become disorganized and dysfunctional; many are replaced or crowded by scar tissue; Massage is: **absolute contraindication**.

**Crohn Disease** is a progressive inflammatory condition that may affect any part of the **GI tract**, from the mouth to the anus; it is characterized by deep ulcers, scarring, and the formation of fistulas around the small and large intestine; Massage is: **acute stage**, **absolute contraindication**; **sub-acute stage**, **indicated**.

**Diverticulosis** is the development of small pouches that protrude from the colon or small intestine; Massage is: **indicated**.

**Diverticulitis** is the inflammation that develops when these pouches become infected; Massage is: **absolute contraindication**.

**Gastroenteritis** is inflammation of the **GI tract**, specifically the stomach or small intestine; Massage is: **absolute contraindication**.

**Gastroesophageal Reflux Disease (GERD)** is a condition involving damage to the lining of the esophagus when it is chronically exposed to digestive juices released from the stomach; Massage is: **indicated**.

**Hepatitis** is inflammation of the liver, usually but not always due to a viral infection; Massage is: **acute stage**, **absolute contraindication**; **sub-acute stage**, **indicated**.

**Ulcerative Colitis** is a condition in which the mucosal layer of the colon becomes inflamed and develops shallow, contiguous ulcers; Massage is: **acute stage**, **absolute contraindication**; **sub-acute stage**, **indicated**.

## Endocrine System

**Addison's disease** – involves the destruction of the adrenal cortex, limiting the secretion of any combination of cortisol, aldosterone, or androgenic hormones; it can be related to an infection but is usually an autoimmune condition; Massage is: **indicated**.

**Cushing's Disease/Syndrome** – is a condition in which cortisol levels in the blood are excessively high for a prolonged period, leading to tissue changes and possibly death; the well-recognized sign of Cushing's Syndrome is the development of fatty deposits around the neck and face and around the abdomen and upper back; Massage is: **indicated**.

**Diabetes Mellitus** – is not a single disease, but rather a group of related disorders that all result in hyperglycemia, or elevated levels of sugar in the blood stream; Massage is: **indicated**, avoid site of injection.

**Goiter** – chronic enlargement of the thyroid gland; may be related to both **hyperthyroidism** and **hypothyroidism**; Massage is: **indicated**.

**Grave's Disease** – is autoimmune hyperthyroidism; antibodies called thyroid-stimulating immunoglobins attack the thyroid gland, causing it to grow to huge dimensions and secrete excessive levels of thyroid hormones, especially thyroxine; Massage is: **indicated**.

**Hyperthyroidism** – is a condition in which the thyroid gland produces excessive amounts of hormones that stimulate metabolism of fuel into energy; Massage is: **indicated**.

**Hypothyroidism** – is a condition in which circulating levels of thyroid hormones are abnormally low; it interferes with the body's ability to generate energy from fuel; Massage is: **indicated**.

## Integumentary System

**Acne** – is a condition of overactive sebaceous glands usually found on the face, neck, and upper back; Massage is: **regional/local contraindication**.

**Athlete's Foot (Tinea Pedis)** – is the most common type of fungal infection diagnosed; it is associated with constrictive footwear and moist, humid conditions; it burns and itches, and may have weeping blisters, cracking, peeling skin; Massage is: **regional/local contraindication**.

**Basal Cell Carcinoma** – is the most common type of skin cancer, accounting for about 80% of all skin cancer diagnoses; it is a slow-growing tumor of basal cells in the epidermis; it usually appears on the face or head; Massage is: **regional/local contraindication**.

**Burns** – first-degree burns are a mild irritation of the superficial epidermis; sunburns are a common version of first-degree burns; Massage is: **indicated**; second-degree burns involve damage into deeper layers of the epidermis; second-degree burns often leave a permanent scar; Massage is: **regional/local contraindication**; third-degree burns penetrate through the epidermis to the dermis or deeper; they destroy skin cells, glands, hair shafts, and nerve endings; Massage is: **regional/local contraindication**.

**Cellulitis** – is a general streptococcal infection of deep layers of the skin; it is a common complication of simple injuries like scraped knee or a contaminated blister from athlete's foot; Massage is: **regional/local contraindication**.

**Decabitus Ulcer** – also called bedsores, are lesions caused by impaired circulation to the skin because of external pressure; this leads to localized cell death and a high risk of secondary infection; Massage is: **regional/local contraindication**.

**Eczema** – is a non-contagious skin rash brought about by a systemic hypersensitivity reaction; it may appear as very dry or flaky skin, coin-shaped lesions, yellowish oily patches, or blistered, weepy skin; Massage is: **regional/local contraindication**.

**Herpes Simplex** – Herpes simplex virus type 1 (**HSV-1**) is associated with lesions that appear around the mouth (oral or respiratory secretions); Herpes simplex virus type 2 (**HSV-2**) is associated with genital herpes (mucous secretions during sexual contact); Massage is: **locally/regionally contraindicated** in the acute stage.

**Urticaria/Hives** – an eruption of itching wheals; Massage is: **absolute contraindication**.

**Impetigo** – is a staphylococcal or streptococcal infection of the skin, it occurs mostly among infants and young children; Massage is: **absolute contraindication**.

**Lice** – a parasite (lice) is any organism that lives by drawing its nourishment from a host, they live on blood or other materials; Massage is: **absolute contraindication**.

**Malignant Melanoma** – **the most dangerous of the skin cancers**; the memory device for identifying melanoma is **ABC**: **asymmetry**, **border irregularity**, and **color change**; melanocytes are the pigment cells deep in the epidermis that give skin its color; age and uneven distribution of melanin in the skin can give rise to several types of skin patches that can become cancerous; Massage is: **absolute contraindication**.

**Moles/Nevi** – are areas where melanocytes replicate, but without threatening to invade surrounding tissues; the melanocytes produce extra melanin causing symmetrical brown, black, purple, blue, or reddish growths with well-defined borders; Massage is: **indicated**.

**Psoriasis** – is a chronic skin disease in which cells, which normally replicate every 28 to 32 days, are replaced every 3 to 4 days; instead of sloughing off, they accumulate into itchy, scaly plaques, usually on the trunk, elbows, and knees; Massage is: **indicated**.

**Ringworm/Tinea Corporis** – is "body ringworm" that typically develops on the trunk or extremities; it generally begins as one small round, red, scaly, itchy patch of skin on the trunk; Massage is: **regional/local contraindication**.

**Acne Rosacea** – is a chronic inflammatory condition involving facial skin and eyes; Massage is: **regional/local contraindication**.

**Scleroderma** – is an autoimmune disorder involving damage to small blood vessels (appears in persons age 30 to 50); it leads to abnormal accumulations of collagen in the skin, blood vessels, and other tissues; Massage is: **absolute contraindication**.

**Squamous Cell Carcinoma** – is a cancer of skin cells related to ultraviolet light exposure that arises in keratinocytes superficial to the basal layer; makes up **one third of all skin cancers**; Massage is: **regional/local contraindication**.

**Warts** – are small, benign growths caused by varieties of human papillomavirus (HPV) that invade keratinocytes deep in the stratum basale of the skin and some mucus membranes; Massage is: **regional/local contraindication**.

## Lymphatic System

**Allergies** – Allergic reactions are immune system mistakes in which an inflammatory response becomes irritating or dangerous as it reacts inappropriately to a variety of triggers; Massage is: **indicated**, except during **acute stage**.

**Chronic Fatigue Syndrome** – CFS is a collection of signs and symptoms that affect many systems in the body and result in potentially debilitating fatigue; Massage is: **indicated**.

**Lymphedema** – is the result of damage to the lymphatic structures and accumulation of proteins in the interstitial fluid; Massage is: **indicated**.

**Lupus** – is an autoimmune disease in which antibodies attack various types of tissue throughout the body; systemic lupus erythematosus is both the most common and most serious; Message is: **acute stage, absolute contraindication; sub-acute stage, indicated**.

**Mononucleosis** – is a viral infection of the salivary glands and throat that then moves to the lymphatic system; the causative agent in about 90% of all cases is the ***Epstein-Barr virus***, a member of the herpes family; Massage is: **absolute contraindication**.

**Edema (Pitting)** - is retention of interstitial fluid due to electrolyte or protein imbalances, or because of mechanical obstruction in the circulatory or lymphatic systems; Massage is: **absolute contraindication**.

## Muscular System

**Adhesive Capsulitis** – or "*frozen shoulder*", is an idiopathic condition in which the connective tissues of the glenohumeral joint capsule and surrounding areas become progressively inflamed, painful, and thickened, which radically limits the range of motion; Massage is: **indicated**.

**Carpal Tunnel Syndrome** – is irritation of the median nerve as it passes under the transverse carpal ligament into the wrist; it affects the thumb, index finger, middle finger, and half of the ring finger; Massage is: **indicated**.

**Fibromyalgia** – is a chronic pain syndrome involving neuroendocrine disruption, sleep disorders, and the development of a predictable pattern of tender points in muscles and other soft tissues; Massage is: **indicated**.

**Golfer's Elbow** – a form of tendonitis, results in inflammation and pain located at the medial epicondyle of the humerus; the flexors of the wrist are affected; Massage is: **regional/local contraindication**.

**Muscular Dystrophy** – is a group of related inherited disorders characterized by degeneration and wasting of muscle tissue; Massage is: **indicated**.

**Strains** – are injuries to muscles involving torn fibers; Massage is: **regional/local contraindication**.

**Temperomandibular Joint Dysfunction** – is an umbrella term that can refer to a multitude of common problems in and around the jaw; symptoms include pain in the head, neck, shoulder, ear, and/or mouth; clicking or locking in the jaw and loss of range of motion of the jaw; Massage is: **indicated**.

**Tendonitis** – is the inflammation of a tendon; it is most common in the tendons crossing the shoulder, elbow, hip, knee, and ankle; Massage is: **regional/local contraindication**.

**Thoracic Outlet Syndrome** – occurs because the brachial plexus and blood supply of the arm become impinged, resulting in shooting pains, weakness, and numbness; Massage is: **indicated**.

**Tennis Elbow** – a common form of tendonitis, results in inflammation and pain located at the lateral epicondyle of the humerus; the extensors of the wrist are affected; Massage is: **regional/local contraindication**.

**Torticollis** – or wry neck, involves a spasm or shortening of one of the sternocleidomastoid muscles; Massage is: **indicated**.

**Whiplash** – or cervical acceleration-deceleration (CAD), is a broad term used to refer to a mixture of injuries, including sprains, strains, and joint trauma; Massage is: **regional/local contraindication**.

## Nervous System

**Alzheimer's disease** – is a progressive degenerative disorder of the brain causing memory loss, personality changes, and eventually death; Massage is: **indicated**.

**Bell's palsy** – is a flaccid paralysis of one side of the face caused by inflammation or damage to **CN-VII**, the facial nerve; Massage is: **indicated**.

**Cerebral Palsy** – is a result of brain damage, usually to motor areas of the brain, specifically the basal ganglia and cerebrum; results in motor impairment, but may also lead to sensory and cognitive problems as well; Massage is: **indicated**.

**Encephalitis** – is inflammation of the brain; it is usually brought about by a viral infection, but other pathogens can cause it as well; Massage is: **absolute contraindication**.

**Hemiplegia** – motor damage from a stroke resulting in full paralysis of one side of the body with complete loss of function; the left or right side (or hemisphere) of the body is affected; Massage is: **indicated**.

**Meningitis** – is inflammation of the meninges that surround the brain and spinal cord; the pia matter is the layer most affected; Massage is: **absolute contraindication**.

**Multiple Sclerosis** – is an idiopathic disease that involves the destruction of myelin sheaths around both motor and sensory neurons in the CNS; Massage is: **absolute contraindication**.

**Paraplegia** – is spinal damage to nerve tissue in the spinal canal that affects the lower abdomen and legs, but leaves the chest and arms intact; Massage is: **indicated**.

**Parkinson's Disease** – the neurons that release the neurotransmitter dopamine in the brain degenerate, thus slowing or stopping its release; dopamine helps the basal ganglia to maintain balance, posture, and coordination; Massage is: **indicated**.

**Quadraplegia** - is spinal damage to nerve tissue in the spinal canal that affects the body from the neck down; loss of movement of all four limbs; Massage is: **indicated**.

**Sciatica** – compression of the sciatic nerves by hypertonic muscles, most commonly the *Piriformis*; results in pain radiating down the leg and may even reach the bottoms of the feet; Massage is: **indicated**.

**Trigeminal Neuralgia** – is a condition involving sharp electrical or stabbing pain along one or more branches of the trigeminal nerve (**CN-V**), usually in the lower face and jaw; Massage is: **contraindicated**.

### Respiratory System

**Asthma** – is the result of airway inflammation, intermittent airflow obstruction, and bronchial hyper-responsiveness; Massage is: **indicated**.

**Bronchitis** – Acute bronchitis is a viral attack directly on the bronchi, although it can also complicate into a bacterial infection; it often accompanies upper respiratory infections or flu; *Chronic bronchitis* involves long-term irritation to the bronchial lining, all the way down to the terminal bronchioles; this can cause the lining to become permanently thick with excessive mucus production that can make it difficult to breathe; Massage is: acute bronchitis, **absolute contraindication**; chronic bronchitis, **indicated**.

**Cystic Fibrosis** – is a congenital disease of exocrine glands that causes their secretions (mainly mucus, digestive enzymes, bile, and sweat) to become abnormally thick and viscous; Massage is: **indicated**.

**Emphysema -** is a condition in which the alveoli of the lungs become stretched out and inelastic; they merge with each other, decreasing surface area, destroying surrounding capillaries, and limiting oxygen-carbon dioxide exchange; Massage is: **indicated**.

**Influenza (Flu)** – is a viral infection of the respiratory tract; Massage is: **absolute contraindication**.

**Pleurisy (Pleuritis)** – is an inflammation of the pleural membrane, usually from a lung infection such as pneumonia; Massage is: **conditionally indicated, physician approval**.

**Pneumonia -** is an infection of the lungs brought about by bacteria, viruses, or fungi; symptoms include coughing that may be dry or productive, high fever, pain on breathing, and shortness of breath; Massage is: **absolute contraindication**.

### Skeletal System

**Ankylosing Spondylitis** – AS is spinal inflammation (**spondylosis**) leading to stiff joints (**ankylosis**); a progressive inflammatory arthritis of the spine; Massage is: **absolute contraindication**, between flares: **indicated**, between flares.

**Baker's Cyst -** also called **popliteal cysts**, are synovial cysts found in the popliteal fossa, usually on the medial side; they may cause pain on knee extension or a feeling of tightness in flexion; Massage is: **regional/local contraindication**.

**Bursitis -** is inflammation of a bursa; a **bursa** is a fluid-filled sac that acts as a protective cushion, eases the movement of tendons and ligaments moving over bones, and cushions points of contact between bones; Massage is: **regional/local contraindication**.

**Dislocation** – is the displacement of the bones of a joint; a subluxation is a partial dislocation; Massage is: **regional/local contraindication**.

**Fractures** – are any variety of broken bone, from a hairline crack to a complete break with protrusion through the skin; the three basic classes are; simple fracture, incomplete fractures, and compound fractures; Massage is: **regional/local contraindication**.

**Gout** – is an inflammatory arthritis caused by deposits of monosodium urate (uric acid) in and around joints, especially the feet; Massage is: **regional/local contraindication**.

**Herniated Disc** – the nucleus pulposus extends beyond the margin of the vertebral body; Massage is: **regional/local contraindication**.

**Osteoarthritis** – is a condition in which synovial joints, especially weight-bearing joints, lose healthy cartilage; Massage is: **regional/local contraindication**.

**Osteomyelitis** – is an inflammation in the bone, bone marrow, or periosteum, usually caused by **pyogenic (pus-producing)** bacteria; the bacteria reach the bone through the bloodstream or by way of an injury in which the skin is broken; Massage is: **regional/local contraindication**.

**Osteoporosis** – is the loss of bone mass and density brought about by endocrine imbalances, poor metabolism of calcium, nutritional, and other influences; Massage is: **indicated**; acute or fragile risks, **absolute contraindication**.

**Rheumatoid Arthritis** – is an autoimmune disease in which the immune system agents attack synovial membranes, particularly of the joints in the hands and feet; Massage is: **regional/local contraindication**.

**Sprains** – are tears to ligaments; in the **acute stage** pain, redness, swelling, and loss of joint function are evident; Massage is: **acute stage**, **regional/local contraindication**.

**Shin Splints** – refers to a collection of lower leg injuries, including muscle injuries, periostitis, hairline fractures, and other problems; they are usually brought about by overuse and/or misalignment at the ankle; Massage is: **indicated**.

## Urinary System

**Cystitis** – is a bacterial infection of the urinary bladder resulting in bloody urine, pain, and increased urination frequency; Massage is: **indicated**.

**Pyelonephritis** – is an infection of the nephrons in the kidney, although the renal pelvis may also be involved; they are usually a complication of a urinary tract infection; Massage is: **absolute contraindication**.

**Uremia** – an excess of urea and other nitrogenous waste in the blood; Massage is: **conditionally indicated, physician approval**.

**Urinary Tract Infection** – a **UTI** is an infection usually caused by bacteria that live harmlessly in the digestive tract finding their way into the urinary tract; Massage is: **indicated** after infection resolved.

## Areas of Caution

<u>**Endangerment Sites**</u> are areas in which nerves and blood vessels surface close to the skin and are not well protected by muscle or connective tissue:

**Inferior to the ear**; notch posterior to the ramus of the mandible

**Anterior triangle of the neck**; bordered by the mandible, sternocleidomastoid muscle, and trachea

**Posterior triangle of the neck**; bordered by the sternocleidomastoid muscle, the trapezius muscle, and the clavicle

**Axilla**; armpit

**Medial brachium**; upper inner arm between the biceps and triceps

**Cubital area of the elbow**; anterior bend of elbow

**Ulnar notch of the elbow**; the "funny bone"

**Femoral triangle**; bordered by the sartorius muscle, the adductor longus muscle, and linguinal ligament

**Popliteal fossa**; posterior aspect of the knee bordered by the gastrocnemius (inferior) and the hamstrings (superior and to the sides)

**Abdomen**; upper area of the abdomen under the ribs

**Upper lumbar area**; just inferior to the ribs and lateral to the spine

Deep stripping over a vein in a direction away from the heart is **contraindicated** because of possible damage to the valve system.

# Special Populations

The best way to obtain information about the special needs of an individual is to ask the client directly. After the practitioner understands the client's particular situation, the physiologic effects of massage that provide the most benefit can be identified and intervention plans can be developed.

**Athlete** - is a person who participates in sports as either an amateur or a professional; two of the most important aspects of sports massage are to assist the athlete in achieving and maintaining peak performance (pre-event & post-event massage) and to support healing of injuries (rehabilitation massage).

**Infants** - most authorities designate babies from birth to 18 months of age as infants; one or both parents must provide informed consent for the massage and must be present during any professional interaction with the infant; in most cases, the contraindications for infant massage is the same as for adult massage.

**Children** - are people ranging from 3 to 18 years of age; due to shorter attention spans than adults, a 30-minute massage usually is sufficient; it is important to only work with children or adolescents with a parent or guardian present.

**Elderly** - persons older than 65-70 years present specific concerns, and appropriate adjustments are required in massage application; it is important to determine if the client is robust (able to function normally and has a great deal of vitality) or frail (unable to function normally, has limited vitality, and has age-associated illnesses); be sure to take a thorough medical history and consider the medications the client is using.

**Clients with Disabilities** - a physical disability or impairment is any physiological disorder, condition, cosmetic disfigurement, or an anatomic loss that affects one or more of the following body systems: neurologic, musculoskeletal, special sense organ, respiratory, cardiovascular, reproductive, digestive, genitourinary, lymphatic, skin, and endocrine.

1. **Auditory/Hearing Impairment** - to get the client's attention, tap him on the arm or shoulder; if no interpreter is present; speak slowly, face the client when speaking; set up hand gestures with the client to reinforce communication before beginning the massage; be sure to read nonverbal clues (fidgeting, moans, or holding of breath); take care when massaging near the ears if the client uses a hearing aid, it may squeal if your hands are too close; maintain contact throughout the massage.

2. **Visual Impairment** - if guiding is necessary, the therapist should walk beside and slightly in front; make sure there is room to accommodate service dogs; be sure to help guide the client up or down stairs and around obstacles; help the client to be aware of their surroundings (where to place clothing and where the massage table and linens are placed); maintain contact throughout the massage.

3. **Limited Mobility/Paralysis** - factors such as injury, illness, pain, or weakness can cause limited mobility; if a client is in a wheelchair, speak with them at eye level; make sure adequate wheelchair access or limited mobility access is available at your place of business; a determination must be made whether to transfer the client onto the massage table, work with him while remaining in the wheelchair or make some other accommodation; make sure the table height is appropriate for the client to safely be helped on and off the massage table; if a client needs to be transferred from a wheelchair to a massage table, the client can give the best directions on how to proceed; avoid any deep techniques or excessive joint movements on a client's paralyzed area; gentle strokes that enhance lymphatic and venous circulation are beneficial for a client with long-term paralysis.

4. **Pregnancy** - pregnant women should receive permission from their doctor or maternity specialists before receiving prenatal massage; massage is **contraindicated** when the woman is experiencing morning sickness, nausea, or diarrhea, or has any vaginal discharge or bleeding; high blood pressure, excessive swelling in the arms or legs, abdominal pain, or a decrease in fetal movement are contraindications for massage and warning signs for immediate referral to a physician; **preeclampsia**, a type of toxemia, is a condition characterized by high blood pressure, edema, and sodium retention; pregnancy increases the chance of **deep vein thrombosis (DVT)** especially in the legs; deep or heavy massage on the legs is avoided during pregnancy; avoid massage on the inside of the ankle because a reflex point in that area stimulates uterine contractions (spleen meridian); massage for pregnant women should be a general massage; watch for fever, edema, varicose veins, and severe mood swings.

5. **Critical/Terminal Illness** - the intent of massage for the critically ill patient is to provide gentle and genuine caring touch therapy to bring comfort, pleasure, and relaxation to someone at a difficult time of life; once the decision to work with someone who is terminally ill has been made, it is important to stay with the process until the client dies, if possible; a critically ill person's physical and emotional condition is constantly changing, constantly assess the client visually, verbally, and tactually, and adjust the massage accordingly.

# Classes of Medications

To help discover what conditions a client might have that could influence the way massage needs to be conducted, massage therapists are encouraged to ask about what medications, prescription or otherwise, their client might be taking.

In many cases, a conversation with the primary care provider is in order to investigate whether the generally parasympathetic changes massage brings about carry any concern or risk in the presence of prescription.

**Anti-anxiety Drugs** - are used to alter the sympathetic "flight or fight" response; they act on the central nervous system (CNS); common side effects include CNS depression, poor reflexes, dry mouth, and feeling unusually exhausted.

**Drug type**: Benzodiazepines (Valium, Xanax)

*Basic Mechanism* - these medications mimic the inhibitory action of the neurotransmitter gamma aminobutyric acid, making neurons harder to activate and suppressing the emotional component of anxiety in the limbic system; used for short term anxiety, seizures, insomnia, and convulsions; Implications for Massage - massage in the presence of these drugs must be conducted conservatively to respect the client's reduced ability to adapt to external changes; using more stimulation may help client avoid dizziness and fatigue at the end of the massage.

**Drug type**: Buspirone HCI (BuSpar)

*Basic Mechanism* - it appears to bind up serotonin and dopamine receptors in the brain, leading to calmer effect without the CNS side effects seen with benzodiazepines; it is less addictive; used for short-term anxiety and for chronic problems like general anxiety disorder; Implications for Massage - clients need to move carefully after a session because of sympathetic suppression and more stimulating massage throughout the session will aid in avoiding dizziness and fatigue.

**Anti-depressant Drugs** - these drugs prolong the availability of various types of neurotransmitters in synapses in the brain; 4 weeks or more are often needed for the drugs to take effect; agitation at the beginning of treatment is common, along with increased anxiety, headaches, and insomnia; other side effects include dry mouth, constipation, reduced sexual function, bladder problems, increased heart rate and dizziness.

**Drug type**: Tricyclics

*Basic Mechanism* - tricyclics block the re-uptake of norepinephrine and serotonin at synapses; this leads to "down regulation" and more normal function of the post synaptic receptors.

Implications for Massage - tricyclics may have dizziness as a side effect; clients may need some gently stimulating strokes at the end of the session to come back to full alertness.

**Drug type**: Monoamine Oxidase Inhibitors

*Basic Mechanism* - MAOIs work by inhibiting monamine oxidase, an enzyme that breaks down the neurotransmitters; the risk of dangerous interactions with some substances, most notably decongestants, and aged cheeses, red wine, pickles, and other foods with tyramine.

**Drug type**: Selective Serotonin Reuptake Inhibitors/Serotonin Norepinephrine Reuptake Inhibitors (Prozac, Zoloft, Paxil)

*Basic Mechanism* - these drugs all work to keep serotonin and norepinephrine present in the CNS synapses for a longer period of time; SSRIs and SNRIs are used to treat various types of anxiety disorders and eating disorders as well as depression.

**<u>Anti- Inflammatory and Analgesic Drugs</u>** - many analgesics work to reduce pain sensation by reducing or inhibiting the inflammatory process; it is important to work extremely conservatively with clients who take these medications because information therapists gather about temperature, muscle guarding, local blood flow, and other signs will be altered and overtreatment is a significant risk.

**Drug type**: Salicylates (Aspirin, Bayer, Doan's Pills)

*Basic Mechanism* - Salicylates inhibit prostaglandin synthesis, which then reduces pain sensitivity and inflammatory response; they also reduce fever by acting on the hypothalamus and promoting peripheral vasodilation; aspirin works to inhibit platelet aggregation.

*Implications for Massage* - reduced pain perception and inhibited inflammation means that compromised tissue may not send a strong signal about pain; bodywork should be conservative to avoid overtreatment and deep tissue massage used with caution; peripheral vasodilation raises the risk for hypotension (dizziness and lethargy) and chilling during and after a massage.

**Drug type**: Acetaminophen (Tylenol, Anacin)

*Basic Mechanism* - these medications act on the heat-regulating center of the hypothalamus to reduce fever; these drugs reduce pain sensation, possibly in both the CNS and in the peripheral tissues.

*Implications for Massage* - caution must be used to avoid overtreatment

**Drug type**: Nonsteroidal Antiinflammatory Drugs (Celebrex, Advil, Excedrin)

*Basic Mechanism* - these medications work to inhibit prostaglandin synthesis at sites of tissue damage to reduce inflammation and pain associated with it.

*Implications for Massage* - NSAIDs are effective for pain and inflammation; they are also associated with stomach and kidney damage; regular use of Vioxx and Celebrex has been shown in some studies to increase the risk of cardiovascular disease, including heart attack and stroke.

**Drug type**: Steroidal Anti-Inflammatories (Cortisone, Hydrocortisone)

*Basic Mechanism* - these all work to undo the main symptoms of inflammation: they reduce pain, heat, redness, and edema in the short run.

*Implications for Massage* - in addition to altering tissue response, they suppress immune system activity; long-term use is associated with weakened connective tissues, fat deposition, muscle wasting, reduced bone density, fluid retention, hypertension, and easy bruising; topical applications of steroid creams can lead to thinning skin; deep tissue massage should not be used when these drugs are used long-term, and myofascial techniques should be used with caution.

**Drug type**: Narcotics and Mixed Narcotics (Codeine, Oxycontin, Vicodin, Morphine)

*Basic Mechanism* - narcotics bind to opiate receptors in the brain to mimic the action of pain-killing endorphins; this leads to a reduced sensation of pain without loss of consciousness, along with suppression of the cough reflex, and gastrointestinal (GI) tract sluggishness; narcotics are potentially addictive.

*Implications for Massage* - deep tissue massage should not be used and stimulation during or at the end of the session is needed to prevent side effects of dizziness and fatigue; avoid massaging around the area of transdermal patches.

**<u>Autonomic Nervous System Drugs</u>** - ANS drugs work to stimulate or block the action of the sympathetic or parasympathetic nervous systems.

**Drug type**: Cholinergics

*Basic Mechanism* - mimic the action of the parasympathetic nervous system.

*Implications for Massage* - care should be taken to not over-treat; these drugs do the exact thing massage does, activate the parasympathetic nervous system; stimulating forms of massage should be used to keep the client alert.

**Drug type**: Anticholinergic Drugs

*Basic Mechanism* - the actions of these drugs vary; they are often organ specific and may suppress or stimulate parasympathetic nervous system receptors.

*Implications for Massage* - looking up the drug, target organ, and side effects, as well as talking with the client about how the drug affects them will help determine if the parasympathetic response is stimulated or blocked.

**Drug type**: Adrenergic Drugs (Dopamine, Epinephrine, Albuterol)

*Basic Mechanism* - these drugs stimulate the sympathetic nervous system.

*Implications for Massage* - inducing a parasympathetic response is more difficult to achieve with the actions of these drugs; longer, slower massages may be needed; be cautious with strokes that stimulate, such as tapotement and friction.

**Drug type**: Andrenergic Blockers

*Basic Mechanism* - these drugs block the action of the sympathetic nervous system at various receptor sites, and include alpha and beta blockers.

*Implications for Massage* - blocking the sympathetic nervous system means the client may be susceptible to going into a deep parasympathetic state with massage; caution should be used to be certain the client is awake and not experiencing dizziness or other effects.

<u>**Cardiovascular Drugs**</u> - work to minimize a sympathetic response or to dilate peripheral blood vessels; when a client uses these substances, their slide into a parasympathetic state may be intensified by massage, leaving the client dizzy, fatigued, and lethargic.

**Drug type**: Beta Blockers (Inderal, Normodyne, Levatol)

*Basic Mechanism* - these affect beta receptors at the heart, bronchi, blood vessels, and the uterus; used to treat angina, hypertension, anxiety, and some other disorders.

*Implications for Massage* - beta blockers can lead to excessively low blood pressure, especially when the client is in a relaxed state.

**Drug type**: Calcium channel blockers

*Basic Mechanism* - these drugs block the movement of calcium ions in smooth and cardiac muscle tissue; the result is vasodilation and more efficient **myocardial** function; used for hypertension and long-term (chronic) angina.

84

*Implications for Massage* - side effects of these drugs include flushing, dizziness, and hypotension; massage should be less emphasis on big, draining strokes and more emphasis on smaller, less circulatory strokes.

**Drug type**: Angiotensin Converting Enzyme Inhibitors

*Basic Mechanism* - ACE inhibitors work by limiting the action of an enzyme that is employed in the renin-angiotensin system: the loop between blood pressure and kidney function; they promote the excretion of sodium and water, reducing load on the heart; used to control hypertension and heart failure.

Implications for Massage - clients may experience fatigue, dizziness, and lethargy if gently invigorating strokes are not administered toward the end of the session.

**Drug type**: Digitalis

*Basic Mechanism* - digitalis increases the force of the heartbeat by boosting calcium in cardiac muscle cells; it also slows the heartbeat through action in the CNS; used to treat arrhythmia and heart failure

*Implications for Massage* - clients who take any form of digitalis to control heart failure are not good candidates for rigorous circulatory massage; invigorating strokes to conclude a session must be chosen to support alertness.

**Drug type**: Antilipemic Drugs (Lipitor, Crestor)

*Basic Mechanism* - cholesterol-lowering drugs work by sequestering bile or by inhibiting cholesterol synthesis; bile sequestering drugs promote the excretion of bile in stool, requiring the liver to use more cholesterol in bile manufacturing; this lowers blood cholesterol.

*Implications for Massage* - a common side effect for all these drugs is constipation as they influence the **GI tract**; if a client has abdominal pain and has had no bowel movement for several days, an acute bowel impaction is possible(medical emergency); other side effects may include muscle soreness, cramping, and weakness; a client with these problems needs a physician's referral; these drugs can cause a life-threatening muscle-wasting disease called rhabdomyolysis; symptoms include worsening muscle pain and weakness.

**Drug type**: Diuretics

*Basic Mechanism* - some diuretics prevent sodium from being reabsorbed in the kidney; as it is processed into urine, sodium then pulls water along with it.

*Implications for Massage* - rigorously applied massage may put an extra load on the kidneys; resting hypotension may also be a problem; general diuretics may cause a loss of potassium that can contribute to muscle cramps.

**Drug type**: Antiangina Medication

*Basic Mechanism* - Antiangina drugs reduce **myocardial** oxygen demand or they increase the supply of oxygen to the heart, or both.

*Implications for Massage* - if a client has a transdermal patch for Antiangina medication, that area and the adjacent tissue must be avoided so that dosage is not influenced; clients have the risk of hypotension, flushing, and dizziness.

**Cancer Drugs** - cancer drugs or chemotherapy drugs are a large group that acts in a wide variety of ways on the body; while the goal is to attack cancer cells, cancer drugs are generally toxic to the whole body; newer drugs can target cancer cells more carefully, but still tax the body as a whole.

**Drug type**: Common Cancer Drugs (Interleukin-2, Interferon)

*Basic Mechanism* - these drugs target the cancer cells and kill them, block the growth of the cells, or block the vascular feeding of the cells.

*Implications for Massage* - always consult a physician; massage application should be very conservative; be aware of methods of excretions (some excrete through the skin) and take appropriate precautions; if radioactive elements are implanted in the body, check with the physician on any limits to the time that should be spent in close proximity to the client.

**Clotting Management Drugs** - medications to manage blood clots come in three basic forms: anticoagulants to prevent the formation of new clots by acting on the clotting factors; antiplatelet medications prevent the clumping of platelets to form new clots; thrombolytics, which are used to dissolve preexisting, clots.

**Drug type**: Anticoagulants (Heparin, Lovenox, Coumadin)

*Basic Mechanism* - these drugs alter the formation of clotting factors in the liver to prevent the formation of new clots; used for people with atrial fibrillation, **a high risk of deep vein thrombosis (DVT)**, or for people using hemodialysis.

*Implications for Massage* - all blood clotting medications carry a risk for bruising, even with relatively light massage; the need for these medications indicates a tendency to form blood clots that may contraindicate all but the lightest forms of bodywork.

**Drug type**: Antiplatelet Drugs (Aspirin, Plavix)

*Basic Mechanism* - these drugs prevent platelets from clumping at the site where a clot might otherwise form.

*Implications for Massage* - the risk of bruising must still be respected for clients who take antiplatelet drugs.

**Diabetes Management Drugs** - when type II diabetes cannot be managed by diet and exercise alone, diabetic management drugs are used and may culminate with the supplementation of insulin; type I diabetes is managed with the use of insulin injections in various forms.

**Drug type**: Insulin

*Basic Mechanism* - insulin is administered by injection, either through multiple daily injections or through an insulin pump; it decreases blood glucose by helping to deliver glucose to cells that need this clean-burning fuel to do their jobs.

*Implications for Massage* - insulin injection sites need to be locally avoided in order not to interfere with normal uptake of the drug; avoid it for 24 hours if the length of time for peak effect is unknown; it is best for a client taking these drugs to receive massage in the middle of their insulin cycle; it may be also useful for a new client to check blood glucose before and after the session; the therapist can plan ahead and have some juice, milk or candy available if needed.

**Drug type**: Oral Glucose Management Drugs

*Basic Mechanism* - these drugs work in a variety of ways to inhibit the production of sugar in the liver, to improve the output of insulin in the pancreas, and to increase the sensitivity of insulin receptors on target cells.

*Implications for Massage* - clients who manage their diabetes with any combination of drugs and insulin must be monitored carefully for blood glucose stability; it is safest to work with these clients after the peak of drug activity.

**Muscle relaxant drugs** - muscle relaxants deal with acute spasms related to trauma or anxiety, or to help with chronic spasticity from CNS damage as seen with multiple sclerosis, stroke, spinal cord injury, or cerebral palsy; they can act on the brain, the spinal cord, or the muscle tissue itself.

**Drug type**: Centrally acting skeletal muscle relaxants

*Basic Mechanism* - these medications are central nervous system depressants; they suppress reflexes that would tighten muscles in response to stretching or damage; used to control painful acute spasms related to trauma or anxiety.

*Implications for Massage* - these drugs interfere with muscle protection reflexes; the risk of overtreatment with deep tissue work, range of motion exercises, or stretching is significant

**Drug type**: Peripherally Acting Skeletal Muscle Relaxants (Dantrium)

*Basic Mechanism* - this drug interferes with calcium release at the sarcomas if reticulum of muscle cells, leading to weaker contractions; used to treat chronic spasticity associated with central nervous system damage.

*Implications for Massage* - a client taking Dantrium will have a compromised stretch reflex and falsely hypotonic muscles; massage must be conducted conservatively.

**Thyroid Supplement Drugs** - hypothyroidism is typically treated with supplements to replace thyroid secretions T3 and T4; Levothyroxine sodium is chemically identical to the thyroid secretion T4, and is meant to be converted to bio active T3.

**Drug type**: Levothyroxine Sodium

*Basic Mechanism* - synthetic thyroid hormones mimic the action of the naturally occurring thyroid hormones to boost protein synthesis in cells, promote the use of glycogen stores, increase heart rate and cardiac output, and increase urine output.

*Implications for Massage* - new users of synthetic thyroid supplements may go through a period of nervousness, agitation, and insomnia, which massage may help to improve; taking synthetic thyroid supplements for a long time probably has no significant side effects, and no implications for massage therapy.

**Drug type**: Desiccated Extract

***Basic Mechanism*** - they mimic the action of naturally occurring thyroid hormones to boost protein synthesis in cells, promote the use of glycogen stores, increase heart rate and cardiac output, and increase urine output.

***Implications for Massage*** - a new user may experience increased anxiety, insomnia, or agitation, all of which **indicated** massage.

**Drug type**: Liothyronine Sodium

***Basic Mechanism*** - these synthetic forms of T3 are prescribed for patients who don't have success with Levothyroxine Sodium; they are meant to mimic the action of naturally occurring thyroid hormones to boost protein synthesis in cells, promote the use of glycogen stores, increase heart rate and cardiac output, and increase urine output.

***Implications for Massage*** - anxiety, insomnia, or agitation may occur until dosage is correctly gauged; massage is perfectly appropriate for clients who supplement thyroid hormones.

## Benefits and Physiological Effects of Techniques that Manipulate Soft Tissue (14%)

### Identification of the physiological effects of soft tissue manipulation

Skillfully applied massage is an effective means of influencing the structures and functions of the body. There are two physical effects of massage, **mechanical** and **reflex**, which can occur separately or together.

**Mechanical effects** are direct physical effects of the massage techniques on the tissues that they contact.

**Reflex effects** of massage stimulate the nervous system, the endocrine system, and the chemicals of the body.

### Effects of Massage on the Muscular System

**Mechanical effects** enhance circulation to and from the muscles, deform sensory and proprioceptive nerve endings, and stretch and compress various connective tissues.

**Reflex effects** relax or reset muscle tone, cause **hyperemia**, and warm the tissues.

Massage is an effective means of relaxing tense muscles, releasing muscle spasms and reducing trigger point activity.

Massage aids in the removal of metabolic waste products and helps to nourish tissues.

Massage prevents and relieves stiffness and soreness of muscles.

Injured muscle tissue heals more quickly with less connective tissue buildup and scarring.

Massage can release fascial restrictions and reduce the thickening of connective tissues (**hyperplasia**), allowing more flexibility and easier, pain-free movement.

**Friction massage**, when properly applied, prevents and reduces the development of adhesions and excessive scarring after trauma.

Massage can have positive effects on the **range of motion (ROM)** of limbs taken through the ROM passively.

### Effects of Massage on the Nervous System

The **sensory nerves** and their **associated nerve receptors** are the nerves that are influenced by massage.

The nervous system can be **stimulated** or **soothed**, depending on the type of massage movement applied.

**Stimulating massage techniques:**

*Friction* stimulates nerves.

*Percussion* increases nerve irritability; strong percussion for a short period excites nerve centers directly; prolonged percussion tends to anesthetize the local nerves.

*Vibration* stimulates peripheral nerves and all nerve centers with which a nerve trunk is connected.

**Sedative effects of massage techniques:**

*Gentle stroking* produces calming sedative results.

*Light friction* and *petrissage* produce marked sedative effects.

Holding pressure (*ischemic compression*) on a sensitive trigger point desensitizes the point and helps to release the pathophysiologic reflex cycle that maintains hypertension in the associated muscle.

### Effects of Massage on the Autonomic Nervous System

The effects of massage on the autonomic nervous system are mostly reflexive.

Initially, massage seems to alert the sympathetic nervous system; short invigorating massage tends to stimulate the body, leaving it more alert and energized.

Longer, relaxing massage seems to affect the autonomic nervous system by sedating the sympathetic nervous system and stimulating the parasympathetic nervous system.

**Effects of Massage on Neurotransmitters:**

Massage reduces the blood levels of the stress-related adrenal hormones **epinephrine** and **norepinephrine**.

Massage has been found to increase the levels of **serotonin, dopamine, endorphins,** and **enkephalins** – **neurochemicals** related to elevated moods and pain control.

Short invigorating massage tends to stimulate the production of **epinephrine** and **norepinephrine**.

A full, relaxing, one hour rhythmic massage decreases the levels of **epinephrine** and **norepinephrine** and encourages relaxation.

Massage increases the levels of available **serotonin** and **dopamine**; results in decreased stress and depression and an elevated mood.

Massage increases the secretions of **endorphins** and **enkephalins** in the CNS; these elements are mood and natural painkillers.

**Epinephrine** – "fight or flight" hormone that prepares the body to respond to emergencies; *epinephrine* functions in the body.

**Norepinephrine** - "fight or flight" hormone that prepares the body to respond to emergencies; *norepinephrine* is active in the brain.

**Dopamine** – is a neurotransmitter that controls fine movement, emotional response, and the ability to experience pleasure and pain.

**Serotonin** – is a neurotransmitter that helps to regulate nerve impulses and influence mood, behavior, appetite, blood pressure, temperature regulation, memory, and learning.

**Effect of Massage on Pain:**

The positive effects of relaxing massage interrupt the transmission of pain sensations of affected **nociceptors** from entering the CNS by stimulating other **cutaneous** receptors (**gate control theory**).

Stimulation of **thermoreceptors** or **mechanoreceptors** by rubbing, massaging, icing, or other means is transmitted along the larger fibers and suppresses the pain sensations at the **gate**, where the fibers enter the spinal column.

Massage also reduces the sensation of pain by increasing the concentration of **endorphins** and **enkephalins** and other pain-reducing neurochemicals in the CNS and bloodstream.

Massage can relieve referred **myofascial** pain and reduce **ischemia**-related pain by releasing hypersensitive **trigger points** and restoring circulation to **hypertonic** muscle tissue.

Techniques such as compression, positioning, stretching, and pressure alter feedback circuits and allow new pain-free possibilities for muscle length and function.

### Effects of Massage on the Circulatory System

•Increased blood flow to the massaged area, better circulation and elimination are favored.

•Blood pressure and heart rate are temporarily reduced.

•Under the influence of massage, the blood-making process is improved, resulting in an increase in the number of red and white blood cells.

**Massage movements affect blood and lymph channels in the following ways**:

*Light stroking* produces an almost instantaneous, temporary dilation of capillaries; deep stroking brings about a more lasting dilation and flushing of the massaged area.

*Light percussion* causes a contraction of blood vessels, which tend to relax as the movement is continued.

*Friction* hastens the flow of blood through the superficial veins, increases the permeability of the capillary beds, and produces an increased flow of interstitial fluid; this creates a healthier environment for the cells.

*Petrissage* or *kneading* stimulates the flow of blood through the deeper arteries and veins.

**Conditions Generally Relieved by Massage:**

Pain in the shoulders, neck, and back (when caused by strained muscles or irritated nerves) is relieved.

Muscles and joints become suppler, and soreness and stiffness are relieved.

Muscle soreness from overexertion can be reduced or prevented.

Muscular spasms are relieved.

Circulation is improved, thus improving delivery of nutrients and the removal of metabolic wastes from the tissues.

Digestion, assimilation, and elimination are often improved.

Facial massage helps to tone the skin, helps prevent blemished skin, and softens fine lines.

Headache and eyestrain are often relieved.

Pain in joints, sprains, and poor circulation are relieved.

Increased circulation of nourishing blood to the skin and other parts of the body encourages healing.

Mildly high blood pressure is temporarily reduced.

Constrictions and adhesions can be reduced or prevented as traumatized muscle tissue heals.

Joint mobility can be increased.

## Psychological aspects and benefits of touch

Stress and tensions are relieved; the client feels better able to cope with day-to-day situations.

Mental and physical fatigue is relieved, leading to renewed energy and ambition.

Deep relaxation is induced, and insomnia is often relieved.

Mental strain is reduced, resulting in better productivity.

Renewed sense of confidence and control is experienced.

## Benefits of soft tissue manipulation for specific client populations

### Elderly Clients

Improved mobility, strength, and flexibility

Improved ability to perform activities of daily living such as dressing, bathing, or climbing stairs

Increased independence

Abdominal massage can help alleviate digestive problems.

Massage helps to ease the anxiety associated with the aging process and helps to provide a social connection with others if loss of friends or family has occurred.

### Infants

Bonding: creation of a close relationship that endures through time.

Relief of tension and pain

Stimulation of several body systems such as circulation and the digestive system (specifically gas, constipation, colic), the immune system, and hormones

Relaxation

### Critically Ill

Helps to control discomfort and pain

Improves mobility

Helps reduce disorientation and confusion by bringing the person back to a more positive body awareness

Reduces isolation and fear

Helps to ease emotional and physical discomforts

Allows the person to develop a more positive attitude about her situation or condition

## Soft tissue techniques

### Types of Strokes/Movements

**Light movements** are applied over thin tissues or bony parts.

**Heavy movements** are indicated for thick tissues or muscular parts.

**Gentle movements** are applied with a slow rhythm and are soothing and relaxing.

**Vigorous movements** are applied in a quick rhythm and are stimulating.

"…the practitioner must pay close attention to the overall response of the client as well as the response of the tissue or body part to which the movement is being applied and adjust the application accordingly."

An important rule of Swedish massage is that most movements or strokes are directed toward the heart (centripetal).

## Description of the Basic Massage Movements

**Touch**: refers to the stationary contact of the practitioner's hand and the client's body; it is the placing of the practitioner's hand, finger, or body part (forearm) on the client without movement in any direction; pressure may vary from light to deep depending on the intention.

**Gliding (effleurage)**: is the practice of sliding the hand or forearm over some portion of the client's body, with varying amounts of pressure or contact according to the desired results.

**Feather-stroking movements** use very light pressure of the fingertips or hands, with long flowing strokes.

**Superficial gliding (effleurage)** is when the practitioner's hand conforms to the client's body contours so that light pressure is applied to the body from every part of the hand.

**Deep gliding (effleurage)** indicates that the movement uses enough pressure to have a mechanical effect.

**Kneading** or **Petrissage**: lifts, squeezes, and presses tissues.

*Fulling* is a kneading technique in which the practitioner attempts to grasp the tissue and gently lift and spread it out; the fleshy body part is gathered up between two hands, then raised and separated by the **thenar eminence** and thumbs as the part is gently stretched across the fibers of the tissue.

*Skin rolling* is a variation of kneading in which only the skin and subcutaneous tissue are picked up between the thumbs and fingers and rolled.

**Friction**: refers to several massage strokes designed to manipulate soft tissue in such a way that one layer of tissue is moved over or against another.

***Superficial friction*** is the application of a brisk effleurage-like stroke using a quick back-and-forth movement intended to warm the area and stimulate superficial circulation.

***Deeper friction movements*** involve moving more superficial layers of flesh against deeper tissues; friction presses one layer of tissue against another layer to flatten, broaden, or stretch the tissue.

***Circular friction*** is movement in which the fingers or palm of the hand move the superficial tissues in a circular pattern over the deeper tissues.

***Cross-fiber friction*** is applied in a transverse direction across the muscle, tendon, or ligament.

***Compression*** is rhythmic pressing movements directed into muscle tissue by either the hand or fingers.

***Rolling*** is a rapid back-and-forth movement with the hands, in which the flesh is shaken and rolled around the axis of the body part.

***Wringing*** is a back-and-forth movement in which both hands are placed a short distance apart on either side of the limb and work in opposing directions.

***Chucking*** involves the flesh being grasped firmly in one or both hands and moved up and down along the bone.

***Shaking*** allows the release of tension by gently shaking relaxed body part so that the flesh flops around the bone.

***Jostling*** involves grasping the entire muscle, lifting it slightly away from its position, and shaking it quickly across its axis.

***Rocking*** is a push-and-release movement applied to the client's body in either a side-to-side or up-and-down direction.

**Vibration** is a continuous trembling or shaking movement delivered by either the practitioner's hand or an electrical apparatus; classified as a type of friction.

**Percussion** or **Tappotement** is a rapid striking motion of the practitioner's hands against the surface of the client's body, using varying amounts of force and hand positions.

***Tapping*** is the lightest, most superficial of the percussion techniques; only the fingertips are used for tapping.

*Slapping* uses a rhythmic, glancing contact with the body.

*Cupping* is a technique used by respiratory therapists to help break up lung congestion; form a cup by keeping the fingers together and slightly flexed and the thumb held close to the side of the palm.

*Hacking* is a rapid striking movement that can be done with one or both hands; the wrist and fingers remain loose and relaxed, and the fingers are slightly spread apart.

*Beating* is the heaviest and deepest form of percussion and is done over denser muscular areas of the body; the hands are held in a loose fist.

**Joint movement**: is the passive or active movement of the joints or articulations of the client.

*Passive joint movements* stretch the fibrous tissue and move the joint through its range of motion.

*Active joint movements* are movements in which the client actively participates by contracting the muscles involved in the movement.

*Active assistive joint movements* are a therapeutic technique to restore mobility in a limb that has been injured; the client attempts the movement, the therapist assists the limb through that movement as necessary.

*Active resistive joint movements* refer to several therapeutic techniques that improve mobility, flexibility, and strength; active resistive joint movements involve movement made by the client that is in some way resisted by the practitioner.

*Active range of motion*: the client moves the limb or the joint without intervention from the practitioner to assess any limitation in the joint movement.

*End feel* is the change in the quality of the feeling as the end of a movement is achieved.

*Hard end feel* is a bone-against-bone feeling.

*Soft end feel* is a cushioned limitation in which soft tissue prevents further movement, such as knee flexion.

*Empty end feel* is an abrupt restriction to a joint movement caused by pain.

**Sequence of application**

**Sequence** refers to the pattern or design of a massage.

The sequence can begin with the client lying face up (**supine**), face down (**prone**), or on either side.

The massage can begin at the head, at the feet, or somewhere in between.

A **Western** or **Swedish-style massage** is designed so that the client only has to change positions once or maybe twice.

A **relaxing**, **wellness massage sequence** is designed so that each body area is thoroughly massaged in a logical order so that the entire body is included and the client feels balanced, complete, and relaxed.

**General Massage Rule**: when doing massage, performing a stroke, or working on an area, work from general to specific.

## Hot/cold applications

The normal core body temperature is 98.6 degrees Fahrenheit. When heat and cold is applied to the body, certain physiologic changes occur.

A short application of cold (**2 to 5 seconds**) has a stimulating effect.

An extended application of cold (**10 to 30 minutes**) depresses metabolic activity.

Local applications have specific local effects; full body applications have systemic effects.

Using thermal treatments below freezing 32 degrees F or above 115 degrees F can damage tissues.

Prolonged general treatments below 70 degrees F can cause **hypothermia**; prolonged general treatments above 104 degrees F can cause **hyperthermia**.

The application of heat causes a vasodilation and a circulation increase in an attempt to dissipate the heat.

Whole-body application of heat causes profuse perspiration, an increase in pulse rate, and an increase of white and red blood cells.

A local application of heat causes a local reddening (caused by vasodilation), increased metabolism and leukocyte migration to the area, relaxation of musculature, and a slight analgesia.

Local applications of cold cause a reduction in nerve sensitivity, circulation, muscle spasms, and spasticity; they have a numbing, anesthetic, analgesic effect; valuable in the relief of pain form bursitis, soft tissue injury, burns, and neuralgia.

**Contraindications**: hot or cold applications should not be given when the client has cardiac impairment, diabetes, lung disease, kidney infection, extremely high or low blood pressure, an infectious skin condition, or open wounds.

**CBAN**: C = cold, B = burning, A = aching, and N = numbness; the four stages of cold application that should be of short duration to prevent tissue injury from freezing.

**Application of cold**: Cold compress, Ice packs, Ice massage, Compressor units with thermal packs and controls, Vasocoolant sprays, and immersion baths.

**Application of heat**: Dry heat (heating pad, infrared radiation, diathermy, and ultrasonography), moist heat (packs and compresses, wraps, sprays and showers, Baths: immersion baths, air baths, steam baths, and saunas).

## Client Assessment, Reassessment & Treatment Planning (17%)

### Organization of a massage/bodywork session

**Note**: *Before performing any massage service, it is important that the client has received adequate information regarding the therapist's credentials, the services offered, and policies and procedures used during the session. It is preferred, and actually required in some jurisdictions, that an informed consent form be signed and kept in the client's file.*

**Informed consent** is an educational process that ensures that the client has received enough information to understand the nature and extent of the massage services.

**First time client or client's first massage**:

Take the client to the massage area; room should be at least **10' x 10' (100 square feet)**; room temperature should be **72 to 75 degrees F**.

Show the client where to hang their clothes and point out the location of the restrooms.

Instruct the client that the best way to receive a thorough and complete massage is with all clothes removed; **give the client the option to leave on whichever clothing feels most comfortable**.

Explain that the genitals and breasts (private areas) will be carefully (modestly) covered at all times.

Demonstrate the massage table, how it is draped, and how the draping works; **only that part of the body being massaged is uncovered at any time**.

Ask about the use of music and offer a few selections.

Ask about lubricant. It is important for clients to choose the type of lubricant or to have no lubricant to avoid any misrepresentation of the therapist diagnosing or prescribing.

Explain that you will leave the room and allow the client the privacy to undress; if the client needs assistance, use a sheet or screen to maintain modesty.

Explain all sanitary precautions.

Show the client the sign on the door stating that a massage is in session and explain why the door is not locked.

Give a general idea of the massage flow; explain what you will do and why.

Instruct the client to get on the table by sitting between the end of the table and the hinged area (portable table) or in the middle of a free-standing table; **a footstool is a useful item to assist the client onto and off the table.**

Explain the requested starting position on the table (**prone**, **supine** or **side lying**); the client should lean to one side to position themselves in the requested position.

Ask the client if they have any questions.

Explain that you will be washing your hands and preparing for the massage while the client gets ready.

Tell the client how long you will be gone and that you will knock and announce yourself before entering the massage area.

**Use bolsters when necessary for the client who has reduced flexibility in the ankles**, **knees**, or **lower back**; under the knees (supine) to place the lower spine in a more relaxed position; place bolster under the ankles when the client is prone; and use pillows in the side lying position; a support under the chest (3" to 4") to take pressure off the cervical spine while in the prone position.

## Client consultation and evaluation

**Verbal intake**: The client consultation or interview is a time to gather and exchange information.

Effective communication begins from the time the client steps into your practice or when you the therapist steps into the client's home or place of business.

If this is the client's first visit, it can be a major component in establishing a trusting relationship.

Greet the client in a professional and friendly manner; make eye contact as you greet the client and welcome them to your practice as you shake their hand.

Ask them their name preference; if it is different than what's listed on your appointment schedule, be sure to make note of it for future reference and follow-up appointments.

**Screening the prospective client with three questions can save valuable time**:

1. What is your previous experience with massage?

2. How did you find out about my services?

3. What is your main reason for making this appointment?

Responses to these questions will clarify whether an appointment is desired and appropriate.

Tell the client before initiating the interview that you would like them to fill out the assembled paperwork (e.g., client intake and medical history, informed consent, and related paperwork).

A well-organized intake form gives both the client and therapist a starting point to engage in dialogue about the upcoming massage session.

After the prospective client has filled out the forms and the therapist has reviewed the information, summarize the information and give the client the opportunity to clarify any information that might need more in-depth consideration.

Communicate on a level with the client and in a manner that the client comprehends.

Discuss any medical information such as high blood pressure or diabetes; find out if it's under control, and what medications if any, the client is taking for that condition.

If the client does take medication, ask how often they take it and what time of day it is taken.

Ask if the client experiences any symptoms or side effects, such as dizziness, fatigue, pain, tingling or numbness, skin problems or bruising, low or high blood pressure.

Clarify the massage session goals and be sure to ask the client for a history of injuries or stressors, and to explain what areas of the body are of greatest concern.

**Be sure to explain and restate your policies and procedures**:

1. **Types of services offered**: list the types of therapy offered, massage benefits, risks, and limitations of massage therapy.

2. **Qualifications of therapist**: provide information regarding licenses, schooling, years of experience, special training, and professional affiliations.

3. **Business policies**: state the policy for appointments, missed appointments, your work schedule, and length of sessions; state that information shared during a session and client files are confidential except when subpoenaed by a court of law; ask the client to sign a Release of Medical Information form before client information is shared for medical or insurance purposes; clearly state your policies regarding sexual boundaries.

4. **Fees**: define the types of payment accepted (e.g., cash, check, credit card, insurance); fee schedule for the lengths of massage sessions or different services.

5. **Massage session procedures**: describe a common massage session and what the client can expect.

<u>**Health history form**</u>

Provides information pertaining to:

1. The client's health history.

2. The primary reason for the appointment.

3. A descriptive profile of the person.

4. A history of the current condition.

5. A history of past illnesses or diseases and health.

6. A history of any family disease.

7. The client's current health practices.

## Written Data Collection

A client database consists of all the information available on which to build the professional interaction, establish client goals, and develop a plan for achieving those goals.

Written data collection is created with information obtained from the client intake and medical history forms, from a history taking interview with the client and other pertinent people, a physical assessment, prior records, and health care treatment orders.

Information obtained during the history and assessment process becomes:

1. The needs assessment and provides the basis for the development of a treatment plan.

2. A means of identifying any contraindications to therapy.

3. An assessment of need for referral.

## Visual Assessment

The observation portion of a client assessment begins when the client walks in the door and continues until the client leaves; how the client holds posture, stands, moves, and sits gives clues to where pain and tension are being held.

**General**: Get a sense of the client's general presence; observe the client's movement and breathing pattern.

Determine if the client displays restlessness, anxiety, fear, anger, agitation, elation, or exuberance (sympathetic dominance).

Or determine if the client has a generally relaxed appearance, contentment, slowness, or depression (parasympathetic dominance); this needs to be considered in the massage's design because therapeutic massage can either stimulate or relax.

Pay attention to where and how a client indicates a problem on his/her body through gestures which often reveal a muscle, joint, or visceral problem.

**Postural**: Ideal posture is when the body's mass is evenly distributed around its central axis, which passes through the body's center of gravity.

Heredity, disease, and habit influence posture; the easiest influence to adjust is habit.

Occupational habits such as a raised shoulder from talking on the phone and recreational habits such as the forward-shoulder position when riding a bike or sleep related habits contribute to habitual postural distortion.

Many postural disturbances are due to agonist/antagonist imbalances; either muscle weakness (flaccidity), muscle tension, or both.

When assessing a client in a standing position be sure to have the client use a symmetric stance; the feet are about shoulder-width apart and the eyes are closed; observe posture when the client is standing comfortably erect from all four sides.

Closed eyes exaggerate most of the client's postural patterns because the client is unable to orient the body visually; if the client tips or rotates their head to feel balanced, this indicates muscular imbalance and internal postural imbalances from positional receptors.

**Lack of Symmetry Landmarks**: the gluteal muscle mass should be even; the tops of the iliac crests should be even; the circumferences of the thigh and calf should be similar on the left and right sides.

The knees should be locked in a standing position, but not be exaggerated; the scapulae should appear even and should move freely; notice if the feet are evenly angled and placed equal distance from the midline and whether the arches support the ankles.

The curves at the waist should be even on both sides; the ribs should be even and springy; the spine should be in a direct line from the base of the skull and on the same plane as the line connecting the nose and navel.

The greater the discrepancy in symmetry, the greater the potential for soft tissue dysfunction.

**Physical**: For a single general massage session, the physical assessment is usually limited to having the client show the therapist any movements that feel restricted or may be causing pain.

Ask client to point out any bruises, varicose veins, or areas of inflammation so you can avoid them.

The massage therapist must ask the question, "Are there any areas that you feel I should avoid?" Be sure the information is indicated on the client intake form.

**Gait**: An assessment for basic therapeutic massage with treatment plan development and agreed-on outcomes over a series of ongoing sessions includes both postural and gait assessment.

**Gait** is a pattern or manner of walking.

It is important to observe the client from the front, back, and both sides; to begin, watch the client walk, noticing the heel-to-toe foot placement; the toes should point directly forward with each step.

The upper body should be relaxed and fairly symmetric; the head should face forward with the eyes level with the horizontal plane.

There is a natural arm swing that is opposite to the leg swing; the rhythm and pace of the arm and leg swing should be similar.

Considerations to observe: Ensure that the gait is initiated without undue pelvic tilt; the feet clear the ground with each step; the foot strikes the ground in a heel-to-toe fashion; the step length is symmetric; straight alignment of the hip, knee, and ankle throughout the entire stride.

## Palpation Assessment

**Palpation** is the use of touch to examine; our hands are our most versatile and exquisite assessment tool.

Palpation is an essential and continuous process, and the hands become skilled with experience.

The main considerations for basic massage are the ability to differentiate between different types of tissue; the ability to distinguish differences of tissue texture in the same tissue types; and the ability to palpate through the various tissue layers from superficial to deep.

Palpation includes assessment for hot and cold, and observation of skin color and general condition; palpation also assesses various body rhythms, including breathing patterns and pulses.

The massage therapist should be concerned with and be able to distinguish the skin, superficial fascia, fascial sheaths, tendons, ligaments, blood vessels, muscles, and bone.

**The Reception Phase** is where the proprioceptors and mechanoreceptors of the hand and arm receive stimulation from the tissue being palpated.

It is best to begin with the lightest palpation and move to the deepest levels; after the hands have been used for deep compression, the sensitivity of the light-touch sensors is momentarily diminished.

The therapist's first impression should be trusted; if the area feels hot, it probably is.

1. **Near-Touch Palpation** does not include touching the body; it detects hot and cold areas.

Done best just off the skin using the back of the hand; the back of the hand is very sensitive to heat; move fairly quickly in a sweeping motion over assessed areas because heat receptors adapt quickly.

Very sensitive cutaneous (skin) sensory receptors also detect changes in air pressure, currents and movement of air.

This is one reason we can feel someone come up behind us when we cannot see him/her.

Being able to consciously detect subtle sensations is an invaluable assessment tool.

Sensitivity or intuition is the ability to work with this information on a conscious level.

2. **Palpation of the Skin Surface** - involves very light surface stroking of the skin.

Determine whether the skin is dry or damp (feel sticky/drags); light stroking causes the root hair plexus that senses light touch to respond.

Notice whether an area gets more goose bumps than other areas (pilomotor reflex); observe color and keep track of all moles and skin surface growths, pay attention to the quality and texture of the hair, and observe the shape and condition of the nails.

3.**Palpation of the Skin** – done through gentle, small stretching of the skin in all directions, comparing the elasticity of these areas; applying light pressure to the skin surface, roughness or smoothness can be felt.

4. **Palpation of the Skin and Superficial Connective Tissue** – petrissage or skin rolling is used to further assess the texture of the skin by lifting it from the underlying fascial sheath and measuring the skin fold or comparing the two sides for symmetry.

The skin should move evenly and glide on the underlying tissues; areas that are stuck, restricted, too loose, or become redder than surrounding areas should be noted.

5. **Palpation of the Superficial Connective Tissue** – which separates and connects the skin and muscle tissue allows the skin to glide over the muscles during movement; found by using compression until the fibers of the underlying muscle are felt; the tissue should feel resilient and springy, like gelatin.

6. **Palpation of Vessels and Lymph Nodes** – just above the muscle and still in the superficial connective tissue lie more superficial blood vessels that feel like soft tubes; feeling for pulses helps detect this layer of tissue.

Lymph nodes usually are located in joint areas and feel like small, soft gelcaps; compression of the joint action assists in lymphatic flow; enlarged lymph nodes should be referred to a medical professional for diagnosis.

7. **Palpation of Muscles** – muscle has a distinct fiber direction that can be felt; feels somewhat like corded fabric or fine rope.

The area of the muscle that becomes the largest when the muscle is concentrically contracted is the belly of the muscle.

Often three or more layers of muscle are present in an area; compressing systemically through each layer until bone is felt is important; the compressive force must be even, broad based, and slow.

Having the client slowly move the joint that is affected can help identify the proper location of muscles being assessed.

8. **Palpation of Tendons** – tendons have a higher concentration of collagen fibers and feel more pliable and less ribbed than muscle; under many tendons is a fluid-filled bursa cushion that assists the movement of bone under the tendon.

9. **Palpation of Fascial Sheaths** – fascial sheaths feel like sheets of plastic wrap; fascial sheaths separate muscles and expand the connective tissue area of bone for muscular attachment.

Fascial separations can be separated by palpating with the fingers; with sufficient pressure, the fingers tend to fall into grooves, which can then be followed.

10. **Palpation of Ligaments** – ligaments are found around joints, are high in elastin and somewhat stretchy; they feel like bungee cords; some are flat.

Ligaments hold joints together and maintain joint space in synovial joints by keeping the joint apart; it is important to be able to recognize a ligament and not mistake it for a tendon.

11. **Palpation of Joints** – joints are found where two bones come together; careful palpation should reveal the space between the synovial joint ends; joints often feel like hinges.

Most assessment is with active and passive joint movements; the sense should be a stable, supported, resilient, and unrestricted range of motion; it is important to assess for end-feel.

12. **Palpation of Bones** – bones feel like young sapling tree trunks and branches; it is important for the massage therapist to be able to palpate bony landmarks that indicate the tendinous attachment points for the muscles and to trace the bones shape.

13. **Palpation of Abdominal Viscera** – the abdomen contains the viscera or internal organs of the body; the massage therapist should be able to palpate the distinct firmness of the liver and large intestine (colon).

Light to moderate stroking of the abdomen is beneficial for the large intestine.

14. **Palpation of Body Rhythms** – body rhythms are felt as even pulsations and are designed to operate in a coordinated, balanced, and synchronized manner.

When a person feels "off" or "out of sync", often he or she is speaking of disruption in the entrainment process of body rhythms.

The **three basic body rhythms** are respiration, circulation, and craniosacral rhythms.

**Respiration**: Palpation of the breath is done by placing the hands over the ribs and allowing the body to go through three or more cycles as the massage therapist evaluates the evenness and fullness of breath.

Relaxed breathing should result in a slight rounding of the upper abdomen and lateral movement of the lower ribs during inhale; movement in the shoulders or upper chest indicates potential difficulties in the breathing mechanism.

**Circulation**: Movement of blood is felt at the major pulse points; palpation of the movement of blood is done by placing the fingertips over the pulse points on both sides of the body and comparing for evenness.

*Vascular refill rate* is another means of assessing the efficiency and rhythm of the circulation; press the nail beds until they push blood out (blanch), then let go and count the seconds until color returns.

**Craniosacral Rhythm**: Also called the Primary Respiratory Mechanism and related cranial rhythmic impulse is a subtle but detectable widening and narrowing movement of the cranial bones.

A to-and-fro oscillation of the sacrum should be noted; palpation of the craniosacral rhythm is done by lightly placing the hands on either side of the head and sensing for the widening and narrowing of the skull.

These sensations normally occur at a rate of 10 to n14 times per minute; movement should feel coordinated and even.

## Range of Motion Assessment

**Active Range of Motion** is performed when the client moves the joint through the planes of motion that are normal for that joint.

Any pain, crepitus (grating feeling or sound), or limitation present during the action is reported; identifies what the client is willing or able to do.

**Passive Range of Motion** is performed when the massage therapist moves the joint passively through the planes of motion that are normal for that joint.

Identifies limitation (*hypomobility*) or excess movement (*hypermobilty*) of the joint; passive range of motion gives information about the joint capsule and ligaments and other restricting mechanisms, such as muscles.

Range of motion is measured in degrees; joint movement is measured from the neutral line of anatomic position.

*Overpressure* is the term used when the massage therapist gradually applies more pressure when the end of the available passive range of joint motion has been reached.

**End-feel** is the sensation transmitted to the therapist's hands by the tissue resistance at the end of the available range.

**End-feel** is the perception of the joint at the limit of its range of motion, and it is either soft or hard.

**Active Assisted Resisted Movement** assesses the relative strength of muscles.

To perform, stabilize the body part in a neutral position near the midrange of the joint and instruct the client to move that body part in a specific direction.

As the client contracts the muscle required to move in that direction, the therapist applies pressure to move the body part in the opposite direction so the limb does not move.

A muscle test that is strong and pain free indicates healthy muscle tissue; a strong and painful muscle test indicates a lesion in the contractile tissue such as a minor muscle strain.

A weak and painless muscle test indicates interference with the nerve supply, circulation, or energy to the muscle; no strength in the muscle could be caused by a severe muscle or tendon (third-degree strain) or loss of innervation.

A very weak and painful muscle test indicates a severe lesion, possibly a torn ligament or fracture that should be referred to a doctor.

## Types of End-Feel

**Normal End-Feel:**

*Soft tissue approximation end-feel* occurs when the full-range of the joint is restricted by the normal muscle bulk; it is painless and has a feeling of soft compression.

*Muscular or tissue stretch end-feel* occurs at the extremes of the muscle stretch.

*Capsular stretch or leathery end-feel* occurs when the joint capsule is stretched at the end of its normal range; it is painless and has the sensation of stretching a piece of leather.

*Bony or hard end-feel* occurs when bone contacts bone at the end of normal range; it is abrupt and hard.

**Abnormal End-Feel:**

*Empty end-feel* occurs when there is no physical restriction to movement except the pain expressed by the client.

*Muscle spasm end-feel* occurs when passive movement stops abruptly because of pain; there may be a springy rebound from reflexive muscle spasm.

*Boggy end-feel* occurs when edema is present; it has a mushy, soft quality.

*Springy block or internal derangement end-feel* is a springy or rebounding sensation in a noncapsular pattern; indicates loose cartilage or meniscal tissue within the joint.

*Capsular stretch* (*leathery*) *end-feel* that occurs before normal range indicates capsular fibrosis with no inflammation.

*Bony* (*hard*) *end-feel* that occurs before normal range indicates bony changes or degenerative joint diseases or malunion of a joint after a fracture.

# Clinical reasoning

**Clinical reasoning** in massage therapy is the process by which a massage therapist, while interacting with a client, formulates meaning, goals, and treatment strategies based on client preferences, client history, and physical assessment, which are in turn informed by the depth and scope of the therapist's knowledge and clinical experience.

**Clinical reasoning** requires that a massage therapist be investigative; using the information gathering process, the massage therapist can discern between similar conditions and make sound decisions about treatment or even decide not to treat the condition at all.

**Ability to rule out contraindications**: The presence of a disease or physical condition that makes treating a particular client in the usual manner impossible or undesirable is called a **contraindication**.

Two categories of contraindications are absolute and local/regional.

**Absolute contraindication** – conditions in which massage is inappropriate, is not advised, and may be harmful to the client.

**Local contraindications** – are those that relate to a specific area of the body; massage may be provided but not to the problematic area.

**Treat as an absolute contraindication**:

If inflammation is widespread or the condition is acute or exacerbated

If the condition is due to an infectious agent or disease

If the condition represents a medical emergency (appendicitis, meningitis)

Until his or her physician can be consulted if the client's symptoms become more severe for any or no apparent reason, which is revealed during the initial assessment

**Treat as a local or regional contraindication**:

If the condition is due to an injury that is less than 72 hours old (e.g., ankle sprain, whiplash)

If pressure causes unwarranted pain; if the area is inflamed (e.g., carpal tunnel syndrome, acute bursitis)

If the area in question is confined to a small space that can be easily avoided (e.g., athletes foot)

If the area presents an abnormal finding such as suspicious moles, masses, or lumps

**Client treatment goal setting**:

Goals describe desired outcomes; problems indicate limits in function; goals reclaim a support function.

Achievable goals often relate to day-to-day activities (functional goals), either personal or work related.

It is important to develop measurable activity-based goals that are meaningful to the client.

Goals must be quantified; they are measured in terms of objective criteria such as time, frequency, 1-10 scales, measurable increase or decrease in the ability to perform an activity, or measurable increase or decrease in a sensation such as relaxation or pain.

Goals need to be qualified; it should be fitted for a given purpose - client will be able to work at the computer for 1 hour (quantified) without pain (qualified).

**Evaluation of response to previous treatment**:

Evaluation involves examining the outcome of the process in relation to the expected goals and objectives.

Evaluation identifies the grounds for altering parts or all of the process to achieve desired results more effectively.

Feedback is a noninvasive, continual exchange of information between the client and the professional.

The massage therapist benefits from feedback about the effectiveness or ineffectiveness of the various massage methods.

Session-to-session reports of progress, post massage sensations and experiences, and the duration of the effects help the massage therapist adjust the application of the massage.

Levels of mobility, pain, posture, and function can be reassessed to indicate the success of the treatment.

**Formulation of treatment strategy**:

Determine if the client has a serious or life threatening condition; if yes refer to medical professional. Rule out any absolute contraindications.

If no, review subjective information on client history to determine what contributed to the client's current situation.

Conduct a physical assessment for objective information of anatomy and physiology that created contributing factors for client's symptoms and outcome goals.

Determine what massage applications would best achieve outcome goals.

Determine the frequency, duration of application and measurement of progress.

Execute Treatment Plan based on the client's individual needs.

## Overview of Massage & Bodywork Modalities/Culture/History (5%)

### History of Massage & Bodywork

**3000 B.C.** – Chinese practiced massage using a special procedure called *anmo* or *amma*.

***Shiatsu*** (by ***Tamai Tempaka***) – is a massage technique using finger pressure from Japan in which points (***tsubo***) of stimulation are pressed to affect the circulation of fluids and ***qi*** (***life force energy***).

**1800 B.C.** – Hindu sacred book ***Ayur-Veda*** (***Art of Life***) included massage treatments.

**Aesculapius** – Greek who founded the first gymnasium.

**Hippocrates** – the father of modern (Western) medicine thought that all physicians should be trained in massage as a method of healing. He used the word ***anatripsis*** in his writings, which mean the art of rubbing upward.

**Aulus Cornelius Celsus** – wrote ***de Medi*** or ***De Medicina***, which describes exercise, bathing and massage.

**Per Henrik Ling** – father of physical therapy; introduced Swedish Movements.

**Charles and George Taylor** – introduced the ***Swedish Movement Cure*** to the United States in New York (1858).

**Dr. Johann Mezger of Holland** – establishes scientific massage as a basis of rehabilitation; preferred the French terminology effleurage, petrissage, tapotement and massage.

**Dr. John Harvey Kellogg** – ran the Battle Creek Sanitarium in Battle Creek, Michigan; wrote extensively on the benefits of massage and hydrotherapy.

**Drs. Emil and Astrid Vodder** – introduce ***Lymphatic Drainage massage*** in Paris in 1936.

**Elizabeth Dicke** – introduces ***Bindegewebsmassage*** or ***Connective Tissue Massage*** in Germany in 1940.

**Dr. James H. Cyriax** – popularized ***Deep Transverse Friction Massage*** in 1952.

**American Massage Therapy Association (AMTA)** – oldest national professional massage association established in Chicago in 1943.

**Randolph Stone** – developed ***Polarity Therapy*** to balance the body both physically and energetically.

**Dr. Ida Rolf** – developed ***Rolfing***; aligns the major body segments through manipulation of fascia or the connective tissue.

**Eunice Ingham** – systemized Reflexology that focuses on the hands and feet; ***Dr. William Fitzgerald*** is credited with demonstrating the effects of reflexology.

**Dr. Milton Trager** – developed the ***Trager method*** which uses movement exercises called mentastics and gentle shaking.

**Touch for Health** – developed by ***Dr. John Thie*** is a simplified form of applied kinesiology to relieve stress on muscles and internal organs.

**Neuromuscular techniques** – **origin**ated in Europe around 1940 with osteopaths ***Drs. Stanley Lief*** and ***Boris Chaitow***.

**Craniosacral therapy** – developed by ***Dr. John Upledger***; enhances the functioning of the craniosacral system.

**Trigger point therapy** – developed by ***Janet Travell*** in the 1950s.

**David Palmer** – popularized ***Chair Massage*** in 1985.

## Overview of the Different Skill Sets Used in Contemporary Massage/Bodywork Environments

### Characteristics of Common Practice Settings

The massage skills that you learned in school are, in most cases, going to transfer across nearly all work settings. In many cases, what is needed is what you have learned to do: relieve symptoms of stress, reduce anxiety, and manage pain, just to name a few.

Massage therapy happening in a spa, healthcare facility, sports facility, or in a private practice setting is primarily defined by location, not the type of massage therapy being performed. Some of the specific differences include:

**Injury Rehabilitation:** Massage therapy for injury rehabilitation will likely take place in a healthcare work setting. The ***physical space*** may include medical equipment and other staff. The massage therapist will usually not have control of the ***climate***. The massage therapy session may take place in a brightly lit hospital room where frequent interruptions are likely. In many cases the massage therapy session will be performed while the client/patient is lying in bed or perhaps sitting in a wheel chair.

Strong interpersonal skills are necessary for success in healthcare environments because massage therapists are part of a larger team. Superior communication and written skills are necessary because you will be expected to document or chart the work you do with a client/patient.

**Sports Massage:** Depending on the sport or event, the ***physical space*** could be outdoors with a table under a tent or it could be indoors in a training or locker room. The ***climate*** for outdoors will be dictated by current weather conditions and indoors might include other therapists working in close proximity or on-lookers such as the press, coaches, or other athletes.

You will need to understand the role of other healthcare practitioners, become familiar with the standard treatment protocols, and be able to effectively communicate with the other healthcare team members using the correct terminology.

**Relaxation:** A relaxation massage can take place in a spa, private practice, on a cruise ship, in a hotel, or at a client's home. In most cases the ***physical space*** will be in a separate room free of distractions. The therapist has more control of the ***climate*** because the lighting and temperature can be adjusted and the possibility of interruptions is limited.

Working in a spa setting can be intense. ***Time management*** and ***self-care*** are of extreme importance because you may find yourself with back-to-back appointments and short breaks between sessions. Strong communication skills are required to be able to communicate effectively with clients, fellow staff, and supervisors.

## General Scope of Practice

**Professionalism:** A Massage Therapist must provide first-rate levels of professional therapeutic massage and bodywork services and demonstrate excellence in practice by promoting healing and well-being through responsible, compassionate and respectful touch.

**Legal and Ethical:** A Massage Therapist must comply with all the legal requirements in his or her local and state jurisdiction that regulates the profession of therapeutic massage and bodywork.

**Confidentiality:** A Massage Therapist must respect the confidentiality of client information and safeguard all records.

**Business Practices:** A Massage Therapist shall practice honesty, integrity, and lawfulness in the business of therapeutic massage and bodywork.

**Roles and Boundaries:** A Massage Therapist shall adhere to ethical boundaries and maintain the professional role designed to protect both the client and the practitioner, and safeguard the therapeutic value of the relationship.

**Sexual Misconduct:** A Massage Therapist must refrain from any behavior that sexualizes, or appears to sexualize, the client/therapist relationship.

## Referring to Other Healthcare Professionals

It is important that you refer clients to other healthcare professionals or other massage therapists. If any of the below conditions exist, then consider referring them.

1. The client verbally tells you about a condition outside of your scope of practice.

2. The client's health history raises a red flag.

3. You observe something during the massage.

4. The client asks you to use techniques outside of your level of training or comfort zone.

5. You are unable to maintain appropriate boundaries.

6. If you feel there is bad chemistry between you and the client or a feeling that you are not safe.

## Ambiance and Approach

Creating an environment that makes the client feel comfortable in anticipation of their massage is a basic tenet of a successful massage practice.

The way you greet and connect with clients, how you obtain information and history, and how you help clients understand how the techniques used during the session will address their issues significantly affect the session and the clients' overall experience.

1. The sights, sounds, and smells that a client encounters create the ambiance and affect the client's expectations.

2. In order to create a relaxing environment, adequate indirect lighting should be used to ensure the physical and psychological safety of your clients.

3. The massage room should be clean, warm (72-75 degrees F), and well-lit. There should be a place for the client to comfortably sit, an area to put their clothes and personal items, and have easy access to a bathroom.

4. Greet your clients with a warm smile and firm handshake. This will help the clients relax and feel welcomed.

5. Ask the client if they have a preference for a particular selection of music.

6. Clients are able to relax more if you inform them how the massage will start and progress. Be sure to find out what areas need more attention and if there are any areas to avoid.

7. Ask the client if they would like to end the session with some assisted stretching or range-of-motion movements and explain how this will benefit their goals.

8. Close the session by offering the client a bottle of water. Explain to the client what you did during the session, what they may experience later that day or the next, and work with the client to develop a plan of continued treatment if needed.

9. Instead of asking a client to rebook, set an expectation. "Let's schedule your next appointment two weeks from now so we can continue with the stress and pain management."

10. Remember to assign or remind your clients of any homework such as daily stretching exercises or to follow-up after their next doctor's appointment.

## Overview of Massage/Bodywork Modalities

### Western massage/bodywork modalities

**Swedish** – employs the traditional manipulative techniques of effleurage, petrissage, and tapotement. It works mainly on the muscles, tendons, and ligaments, and increases the body's blood and lymphatic circulation. It usually induces a state of deep relaxation.

**Deep Tissue** – releases the chronic patterns of tension in the body through slow strokes and deep pressure on contracted areas, both by following and going across the grain of muscles, tendons, and fascia.

**Sports Massage** – is a massage technique designed specifically for athletes or those who engage in a sports, exercise, or fitness program. It is usually deeper and more vigorous than an average massage. It is used prior to activity (***pre-event***) and/or after (***post-event***) to assist the body in recovering from the aftereffects of such an activity.

**Trigger Point Therapy** or **Neuromuscular Therapy** – applies concentrated finger pressure to "***trigger points***", which are painful, irritated areas in muscles, to break the cycle of spasm and pain.

**Reflexology (zone therapy)** – systemized by *Eunice Ingham*, is organized around a system of points on the **hands** and **feet** that are thought to correspond to major joints and organs of the body.

**Manual Lymphatic Drainage (MLD)** – *Dr. Emil* and *Astrid Vodder* developed MLD to stimulate lymph flow and fluid movement using light, rhythmic strokes. Used for inflammation, lymphedema, and circulatory disturbances.

**Polarity Therapy** – developed by *Dr.Randolph Stone* in the 1950s, is based on the idea that the body has an electromagnetic field that can be balanced by gentle rocking movements and specific hand placements. Polarity therapy is an energy-based healthcare system that incorporates diet, exercise, and self-awareness into its practice.

**Chair Massage** – popularized by *David Palmer*, is performed on-site, at an office or an event, with the fully clothed client seated in a specially designed chair. Seated massage treatments last between **ten** and **thirty minutes** and often focus on the neck, shoulders, back, arms, and hands of the client.

**Hellerwork/Rolfing** – developed by *Joseph Heller* and *Ida Rolf* respectively, are methods of structural integration focused to bring the physical structure of the body into an efficient relationship with the perpendicular alignment of the body in gravity. The focus is normalization and redirection of the deeper fascial components of muscles and fascial sheaths.

**Craniosacral Therapy** – developed by *Dr. John Upledger*, treats the bones and membranes surrounding the brain and spinal cord to free restrictions in the flow of cerebrospinal fluid, increasing overall health and relieving pain and stress.

**Myofascial Release** – developed by *John Barnes* in the 1970s, provides gentle stretching and elongation of the connective tissues in and around the muscles, especially at trigger points. This therapy restores balance, health, and elasticity while relieving pain.

**Lomilomi** – a massage technique that originated in Hawaii that mostly uses the forearms to knead, rub, and weave like a dance; it aligns the body, mind, and spirit.

**Reiki** – a system of treatment that channels universal healing energy through the practitioner's hands into and around the client's body, sometimes without direct hands-on application.

**Aromatherapy** – is the use of essential oils processed from herbs, flowers, fruits, stems, spices, and roots in massage, inhalation, or other modalities to affect mood and improve health and well-being.

**Hydrotherapy** – is the application of water in any of its three forms (solid, liquid, and vapor) to the body for therapeutic purposes.

**Ortho-Bionomy** – developed by *Arthur Lincoln Pauls* is a healing system based on the body's self-correcting reflexes; *Ortho* means to correct or straighten; *Bionomy* is the study of life processes.

## Eastern massage/bodywork modalities

**Shiatsu (finger pressure)** – from Japan is a form of massage in which the fingers are pressed onto particular points of the body to ease aches, pain, tension, fatigue, and symptoms of disease. The points are called *tsubo*, or *acupuncture points*, and are located along **(12) meridians** or pathways.

**Ayurveda** - means *life knowledge* or *right living*. It is grounded as a body/mind/spirit system in the Vedic scriptures. The **tridosha theory** is unique to this system. A *dosha* is a body chemical pattern. The **three doshas** are *Vata* (wind), *Pitta* (bile), and *Kapha* (mucus). These three combine to form five elements of ether, air, fire, water, and earth. When they combine, they constitute the nature of every living organism. The points (about 100) connected with this system are called marmas. **Marmas** are concentrated at the junctions of muscles, vessels, ligaments, bones, and joints. These junctions form the seat of **vital life force (Prana)**.

**Thai massage** – An ancient system of massage that includes stimulation of pressure points, energy work, and yoga-like stretching to improve health and well-being. Client remains clothed.

# Ethics, Boundaries, Laws, Regulations (15%)

## Ethical Behavior

**Ethics** is the study of the standards and philosophy of human conduct and is defined as a system or code of morals of an individual person, a group, or a profession.

**Ethics** are an individual's or group's standards of behavior.

*To practice good ethics is to be concerned about the public welfare, the welfare of individual clients, your reputation, and the reputation of the profession you represent.*

<u>Ethical Principles</u> - The following eight principles guide professional ethical behavior:

**Respect** – Esteem and regard for clients, other professionals, and oneself

**Client autonomy** and **self-determination** – The freedom to decide and the right to sufficient information to make the decision

**Veracity** – The right to the objective truth

**Proportionality** – The principle that benefit must outweigh the burden of treatment

**Nonmaleficence** – The principle that the profession shall *do no harm* and prevent harm from happening

**Beneficence** – The principle that treatment should contribute to the client's well-being

**Confidentiality** – Respect for privacy of information

**Justice** – Equality

## Professional Boundaries

**Professional boundaries** are the limits of acceptable professional behavior.

**Boundaries** delineate personal comfort zones, the realm in which people operate with a sense of safety and control.

**Boundaries** help to screen input about what is appropriate for our personal comfort.

**Professional boundaries** are predetermined practices that protect the safety of the client and therapist.

**Sexual boundaries** are defined as limits to prevent ever sexualizing any aspect of bodywork.

<u>**Eight Major Areas to Consider in Establishing Professional Boundaries**</u>

**Location** refers to the therapeutic setting where the massage takes place; consideration must be taken to ensure safety, comfort, and security for the client and a sense of professionalism from the practitioner that inspires confidence and respect.

**Interpersonal space** refers to the actual space maintained between the client and practitioner during interactions before and after the actual massage; carry on conversations at eye level whenever possible; discussions that take place when both persons are at the same height minimize the power differential.

**Appearance** refers to the way the practitioner looks and dresses when providing or promoting massage; professional appearance includes appropriate clothing and personal hygiene.

**Self-disclosure** – pertinent information regarding training, experience, modalities practiced, treatment plan, appointment policies, and fees are necessary to gain informed consent and confidence from the client; any personal information should benefit the client and the therapeutic goals of the session.

**Language** – choice of words, voice intonation, and overall skills as a communicator are vital aspects of creating effective boundaries.

**Touch** – quality and depth of touch should be discussed before the session begins and included in the informed consent; touch that goes beyond or deviates from what was discussed in the original informed consent must be clear and completely disclosed to the client so the client can once again give informed consent.

**Time** – beginning and finishing sessions on time honors professional and personal boundaries; establishing and maintaining policies regarding session length, late arrivals, no shows, and missed appointments define boundaries, letting clients know what to expect.

**Money** – the amount of the fee is determined based on the service provided and should directly reflect the value of the service; clients challenge boundaries by not bringing money or a check to pay for a session, by writing a check with insufficient funds, by being late paying, or by not paying the bill at all.

## Code of Ethics Violations

Sexual abuse of clients

The inability to exercise sound professional judgment

Theft from clients or businesses

Practicing without a license or under false pretenses

Substance abuse

## The Therapeutic Relationship

**The Therapeutic Relationship** is a practitioner/client relationship that is client centered, in which all activities benefit and enhance the client's well-being and maintain or promote individual welfare.

**Create a safe environment**, a place where any client is secure enough to allow healing to occur; a place that is safe enough to be vulnerable, to be open, to release, to relax, be nonthreatened; a place of trust or a safe haven in which to unwind.

**Confidentiality** is the principle that the client's information is private and belongs to the client; even when the client's name is withheld; the situational uniqueness often is enough to breach confidentiality requirements.

**Confidentiality** in the practitioner/client relationship is the foundation of safety, protection, trust, and respect; clients should not be acknowledged in public unless they recognize and greet the professional first.

**Confidentiality** provides an environment of safety, trust, and respect for the client to heal and relax.

•The practitioner keeps all personal information regarding any client, including the fact of being a client, private *except with the permission of the client or in certain circumstances required by law*.

**The duty to warn and protect** is a legal requirement that the practitioner report to authorities situations of imminent or life-threatening danger by or to a client or situations of child abuse.

**Power differential** is evident in which more authority is held by the person on one side of the relationship (therapist), whereas the other person is in a more vulnerable or submissive role (client).

**Establishing a policy** early in the therapeutic relationship that encourages the client to speak up anytime there is discomfort (*signs of discomfort: withdrawal or fidgeting*) of any kind during the course of treatment empowers the client to better direct the experience and reduces the likelihood of personal boundaries being severely crossed.

**Transference** is the personalization of the professional relationship by the client, either positively or negatively, by unconsciously projecting characteristics of someone from a former relationship onto the therapist.

**Signs of Transference**: *Transference* occurs when the client sees the therapist in a personal light instead of a professional manner.

Client asks personal questions not related to the reason for the visit

Client might vie for extra time during or at the end of the session

Client brings or offers gifts

Client proposes friendships or sexual involvement

Client might invite the practitioner to social activities

**Countertransference** happens when a therapist personalizes a therapeutic relationship by unconsciously projecting characteristics of someone from a former relationship onto a client.

<u>**Signs of Countertransference**</u>: Countertransference presents itself in feelings of attachment to the client.

Fantasizing or having sexual feelings toward a client

Excessive thinking about a client between visits

Spending extra time with a client

Feeling guilty, frustrated, or angry if a client does not respond to treatment

Feeling anger or disappointment if a client is late or cancels

## Dual Relationships

**Dual Relationships** is any situation that combines the therapeutic relationship with a secondary relationship that extends beyond the massage practitioner/client relationship.

The relationship begins when a prospective client makes an appointment and comes in for a session; an attraction, one for the other or mutual, results in a social or romantic relationship beyond the therapeutic relationship.

The professional is ultimately responsible for maintaining boundaries.

**Dual relationships** are a normal part of human interaction, but are nearly always detrimental to the therapeutic relationship.

Because of the ***power differential*** in the therapeutic relationship, it is the practitioner's responsibility to act ethically.

# Sexual Misconduct

The massage professional must understand the physiologic aspects of therapeutic massage and recognize that the same massage techniques that alleviate stress and promote relaxation also stimulate the entire sensory mechanism, which may include a sexual arousal response.

*The entire arousal response is part of the relaxation response via the output from the parasympathetic autonomic nervous system.*

*Each time a client relaxes out of the fight-or-flight responses of the sympathetic autonomic nervous system into a more relaxed response, the predisposing physiologic factors are present for sexual arousal.*

<u>**Sexual Misconduct includes the following**</u>:

Any behavior, gestures, or expressions that is seductive or sexually demeaning to a client

Draping practices that reflect a lack of respect for the client's privacy

Conversations about the sexual preferences or fantasies of the client or massage therapist

Touching or undraping the genitals or breasts

Engaging in any conduct with a client that is sexual or reasonably may be interpreted as sexual

Sexual comments about a client's body or underclothing

# Massage/Bodywork-Related Laws and Regulations

*The main purpose of a law or an ordinance is to protect the safety and welfare of the public.*

Most licensing laws contain educational, technical, ethical, and sanitation requirements.

In the United States 43 states and the District of Columbia license massage therapists.

Must be at least 18 years of age, be a high school graduate, complete a ***minimum of 500 to 1000 hours*** of massage therapy training from a school or program recognized by the board.

In 2007, the Federation of State Massage Therapy Licensing Boards (FSMTB) created the ***Massage and Bodywork Licensing Examination*** (***MBLEx***) as a valid, reliable entry-level competency examination.

A massage therapist cannot diagnose illness or prescribe medication or medical intervention.

A massage therapist can perform a variety of assessments to determine which therapeutic modalities are most appropriate for soft tissue conditions that a client might have or refer to another professional.

Massage establishments must abide by local laws, rules, and regulations; they must be licensed and employ only licensed practitioners and display their licenses.

The massage therapist should be physically and mentally fit and be free of any communicable diseases.

A *license* is issued by a *state* or *municipal regulating agency* as a requirement for conducting a business or practicing a trade or profession.

A *certification* is a document that is awarded in recognition of an accomplishment or achieving or maintaining some kind of standard.

The local government regulates where the professional may work through *zoning ordinances*; local governments are most concerned with what types of activities go on in their region and the way the land is used (*zoning*).

In states that license massage professionals, the practitioner must still comply with *local zoning ordinances* (usually in an area of office or commercial zoning) and building requirements.

Cities adopt ordinances to curb unethical practices, misleading advertising, and the use of the term massage to conceal questionable or illegal activities, especially prostitution or illegal drug sales and distribution.

## Scope of Practice

**Scope of practice** defines the rights and activities legally acceptable according to the licenses of a particular occupation or profession.

**Scope of Practice** defines the tasks that healthcare providers are legally permitted to perform as allowed by state and federal law.

A person may not dispense therapeutic or medical advice about the effect of his or her services on a specific disease, ailment, or condition unless that person has adequate training, knowledge, and experience to ensure that the advice given is sound and reliable.

You can determine if you are within your scope of practice by making sure your responses to the client are from a body and massage perspective.

Each professional has personal limits to his or her *scope of practice*; these limits involve the *type and extent of one's education, personal biases, life experiences, choice of preferred clientele and physical stature and endurance*.

# Professional Communication

**Communication** is the act of exchanging thoughts, feelings, and behavior.

**Communication skills** are required to retrieve information, maintain charting and client records, and provide information effectively so that the client can give informed consent.

**Nonverbal communication (body language)** is how a person's posturing, gestures, and facial expressions provide information about his mental, emotional, or physical condition.

The strongest message is delivered through the **kinesthetic mode** or **body language**; it is important that congruence exist between what is heard, what is seen, and what is felt.

The **practitioner's body language** should send the message that the practitioner is **open, friendly, confident**, and **professionally** interested in the client.

The **tone of voice** is more important than the words spoken; **tone is kinesthetic** and **auditory** because of the pressure waves emitted; we hear and feel the sound waves from the tone of voice.

The **words are the least effective part of the communication pattern**; words can have mixed meanings, depending on each person's definition of a particular word.

Almost everyone processes visual and auditory messages through the kinesthetic mode; the most common pattern is **visual/kinesthetic (see and feel)** or **auditory/kinesthetic (hear** and **feel)**.

**Effective listening** occurs when we listen to understand instead of to respond; **reflective listening** involves restating the information to indicate that you have received and understood the message.

**I-messages** share feelings and concerns; **You-messages** put a person down, blame, criticize, and provoke anger, hurt, embarrassment, and feelings of worthlessness.

**I-Message Pattern**: Describe the behavior or problem you find bothersome (Facts); State your feelings about the situation (Impact on people); State the consequence (Logical cause and effect); Request the preferred behavior or action (Possibilities).

**Open-ended questions** encourage the sharing of information and cannot be easily answered in one word; they begin with **where, when, what, how**, and **which**; avoid why questions because they encourage defensive reactions.

**Communicate** on a level with the client and in a manner the client comprehends.

**Clearly** stating policies concerning missed or late appointments, payment of fees and sexual boundaries avoids misconceptions and awkward situations; **policies can be posted, printed on intake forms or stated verbally**.

Being able to answer the client's questions adds to the practitioner's credibility as a professional and helps to build client confidence.

## Confidentiality

**Confidentiality** guarantees the nondisclosure of privileged and private information that is shared during a therapeutic session.

The identity of a client or any information about them or their condition is kept private and not divulged to any third party.

**Confidentiality** in the practitioner/client relationship is the foundation of safety, protection, trust, and respect; clients should not be acknowledged in public unless they recognize and greet the professional first.

**Confidentiality** is the principle that the client's information is private and belongs to the client; even when the client's name is withheld; the situational uniqueness often is enough to breach confidentiality requirements.

**Confidentiality** provides an environment of safety, trust, and respect for the client to heal and relax.

**HIPAA** (Health Insurance Portability and Accountability Act of 1996) compliance is required by any agency or individual person who stores or transmits personal health information electronically.

Although a massage therapist may not need to be HIPAA compliant, they can strive to follow the guidelines to maintain a client's trust and privacy.

1. Always obtain a signed informed consent before proceeding with treatment.

2. Do not divulge client information to any third party without first obtaining a release of information form signed by the client.

3. Store client files in a secure (lockable), fireproof cabinet.

4. Keep client files and appointment books out of view of others.

5. Protect electronic files with appropriate passwords; use appropriate firewalls when connected to the internet.

6. Ensure that your clients receive **Privacy Policies** that explain how their information will be used, stored and under what conditions it can be shared.

## Principles

A **principle** is a basic truth or rule of conduct.

**<u>Standards of practice</u>** are principles that serve as specific guidelines for directing professional ethical practice and quality care:

Respect all clients, colleagues, and health professionals through nondiscrimination.

Perform only those services for which they are qualified and honestly represent their education, certification, professional affiliations, and other qualifications.

Respect the scope of practice of other health care and service professionals.

Avoid false claims about the potential benefits of the techniques rendered, and educate the public about actual benefits of massage.

Provide a safe, comfortable, and clean environment.

Maintain clear and honest communication with clients and keep client communications confidential.

Keep accurate records and review the records with the client.

Never engage in any sexual conduct, sexual conversation, or any other sexual activities involving clients.

Charge a fair price for the session.

Maintain a professional appearance and demeanor by practicing good hygiene and dressing in a professional, modest, nonsexual manner.

Undergo periodic peer review.

Practice honesty in advertising, promoting services ethically and in good taste and advertising only techniques for which the professional is certified and adequately trained.

# Guidelines for Professional Practice (13%)

## Proper and safe use of equipment and supplies

In a massage therapy work space, it is a good goal to create an environment where nothing that one client touches directly or indirectly is touched by another client before it is cleaned.

Any fabric item (linens, face cradle covers, bolsters, and pillow covers) that a client contacts should be laundered before another client touches it.

Any item that a massage therapist touches during a session with one client should be cleaned or re-covered before it is used again.

When laundering, good anti-microbial effect is found with temperatures from 71degrees F to 77 degrees F (21.6 degrees C to 25 degrees C), if the detergent is strong and is used according to manufacturers' directions.

Bleach becomes most active at temperatures above 135 degrees F (62.7 degrees C); the recommended amount of bleach is a ratio of 50 to 150 ppm (parts per million).

Bleached laundry must be thoroughly rinsed to minimize irritation to users.

Laundry must not be left damp for any significant length of time.

All laundry should be dried on high heat (160 degrees F, 71.1 degrees C).

Clean laundry must be packaged to keep it clean until its next use; it can be wrapped inlays tic or stored in a clean disinfected container.

Adding bleach will shorten the life of fabrics; chlorine bleach does not have an anti-microbial effect; washing with strong detergent and drying with high heat are sufficient for most situations.

Massage tables and chairs can be swabbed with disinfectant between clients; use at least an intermediate-level disinfectant; the CDC recommends a 10% bleach solution on high touch surfaces.

Massage lubricants must be kept free from the risk of cross contamination; liquid lubricants must be dispensed in bottles that are washed between every session.

Lubricants that are solid at room temperature (beeswax, coconut oil) must be dispensed into individual containers and leftovers discarded.

Hot or cold stones and crystals may be the only massage tools that lend themselves to full sterilization; these may be boiled or baked between uses to ensure removal of all pathogens.

Upholstery and carpets should be vacuumed frequently; vinyl or leather upholstery can be swabbed with disinfectant; hard floors can be washed regularly with detergents.

Other surfaces that should be cleaned frequently include doorknobs, bathroom fixtures, light switch plates, telephones, and coat racks or hooks.

## Therapist Hygiene

The primary precaution in infection control is thorough hand washing; *hand washing should continue for at least 15 seconds* to ensure that all surfaces are thoroughly cleansed.

If soap and water are not available, another option is to use an alcohol based (foam or gel) hand sanitizer; sanitizer is applied to one hand and then the *hands are rubbed together for at least 15 seconds until the hands are dry*.

The CDC found that *running warm water plus plain soap for 30 seconds* is adequate for most everyday use; this method is recommended to remove any visible or palpable dirt; it is preferable to dispense soap in liquid form, because bacteria can colonize bar soap.

Fingernails must be kept short and artificial nails should be avoided; hangnails must be kept short and controlled; open lesions on the hands must be covered during a massage (use a liquid bandage or a finger cot).

## Sanitation and cleanliness

There are three main levels of removing pathogens from implements and surfaces: sterilization, disinfection, and sanitation.

**Sterilization** is the most complete process; this destroys all living organisms on an object or surface, including bacterial spores; it is accomplished with baking, steam under pressure, or chemicals under pressure.

**Disinfection** is a medium level of decontamination, nearly as effective as sterilization, but does not kill bacterial spores; it is the destruction of pathogenic micro-organisms or their toxins by direct exposure to chemical or physical agents.

Common disinfectants used today are phenols (Lysol), chlorine bleach, and alcohol.

**Sanitation** is the third level of contamination that is generally done with soaps or detergents and water.

**Cleaning** is the removal of soil through manual or mechanical means.

**Plain soap** is any detergent that contains no anti-microbial products or small amounts of anti-microbial products to act as preservatives.

**Anti-microbial soap** is a detergent that contains anti-microbial substances.

**Alcohol-based hand rub** contains 60% to 95% alcohol (ethanol, isopropanol, or both).

**Universal and standard precautions** are a set of protocols that were introduced in 1987 to create some uniformity in how medical professionals should limit contact with body fluids in the working environment.

**Potentially infectious fluids**: semen, vaginal secretions, breast milk, cerebrospinal fluid, synovial fluid, pleural fluid, pericardial fluid, amniotic fluid, blood, blood tinged saliva, and vomit (**emesis**).

## Safety practices

### Facilities

*Housekeeping/Sanitation*

Keep all halls and walkways clear.

Keep all carpets vacuumed and cleaned.

Keep all solid floors cleaned and sanitized.

Sanitize all restrooms and bathing facilities.

Make sure all floors in wet areas are slip proof.

Sanitize all equipment surfaces that come in contact with clients.

Disinfect hydrotherapy tubs, steam cabinets, shower stalls, and wet tables between each use.

Maintain hand-washing facilities (germicidal soap, sanitary or paper towels).

Linens are commercially laundered or washed in hot water with detergent and dried in a hot dryer; bleach is available and used when there is any chance of contamination.

Clean linens are stored in a closet cabinet; soiled linens are stored in a covered container or stored outside the massage room.

*Equipment*

Check all equipment for safety and stability (tables, stools, chairs)

Each time a table is set up, check all hinges and locks for stability

Maintain all equipment (electrical cords, lubrication)

Store equipment and linens properly

### *Fire Safety*

Maintain functioning smoke and carbon monoxide detectors

Be familiar with the location and use of fire extinguishers

Clearly indicate fire exits

Be aware of and practice evacuation procedures

Establish a policy regarding the use of open flames, candles, incense, and the like

Contact your local fire department for a fire inspection

### *First Aid*

Keep a maintained first-aid kit on the premises.

Make sure that all personnel know the location of the first-aid kit.

As many staff members as possible should learn first aid and cardiopulmonary resuscitation (CPR) techniques.

Keep emergency information posted in plain view near all telephones (fire and police, ambulance, hospital, emergency department, doctors, and taxis).

### *Heat and Ventilation*

Maintain and service heating and ventilation equipment systems regularly.

Use only UL-approved auxiliary heating devices.

Regularly inspect auxiliary heating devices.

Turn off auxiliary heating devices when not in use.

## Therapist personal safety

When lifting equipment or clients, use proper body mechanics and lifting techniques to prevent muscle strain and injury.

Use proper body mechanics and techniques when practicing massage to prevent muscle strain and overuse syndromes resulting in back, shoulder, or arm injury.

Use equipment and adjunctive modalities properly and according to manufacturers' instructions and recommendations.

All practitioners should maintain a current first aid and CPR certification.

Know the location of the first-aid kit.

Wash hands before and after every treatment.

Know contraindications for massage and perform only procedures that cause no injury and are within your scope of practice.

Have a plan in place to deal with or escape from a client who is acting inappropriately or dangerously.

When doing an in-home massage, inform an associate of the location, name of client, time of appointment, and the time you plan to complete the appointment, contact your associate to indicate that you have finished.

### Client safety

***Understand the paths of infection and ensure client's protection with sanitary practices***; **Do no harm!**

Use clean linens with each client.

Wash hands before and after each client.

Provide sanitary bathing facilities and restrooms.

Avoid open wounds and sores.

Do not practice massage if you are ill or contagious.

***Provide safe, clear entryways and passages***

Keep walkways clear and well lighted.

Provide nonskid walkways and floors.

Assist clients on and off of the massage table.

Check to make sure that clients are not sensitive or allergic to products used.

Use proper procedures in dealing with illness and injury; refer to proper medical authorities when conditions indicate.

## Therapist care

**Body mechanics** - means the observation of body postures in relation to safe and efficient movement in daily activities.

Good body mechanics increases the strength and power available in a movement.

Proper positioning of the feet; the strength of the legs; the position of the hips, back, shoulders, and head; and breathing all play important roles in the effective delivery of the massage, the level of fatigue, and the long-term health of the practitioner.

The practitioner who depends solely on the hands and arms will fatigue quickly

Overextending the arms compromises control, force, and pressure.

Overreaching places the back in a strained position due to bending or twisting at the waist

The hands are the practitioner's most valuable tools.

Maintain proper alignment of the wrists by staying behind the massage movements.

Avoid hyperextending the wrist and using the heel of the hand when applying compressive forces.

Use the elbows and forearm when possible to apply deep pressure.

Use the cushioned palmar side of the thumb and fingers rather than the tips when applying pressure with the fingers or thumb.

To reduce strain on the neck, keep the head up, shoulders down and relaxed, and the arms and hands relaxed.

Keeping the hands in good alignment and using body weight and leverage conserves energy and increases the power and strength when performing massage.

Incorporating proper body mechanics and movement enhances the quality, effectiveness, and efficiency of all massage strokes.

Correct posture and stances (foot positions) aid in balance and allow the delivery of firmer, more powerful, and more direct massage strokes.

Correct posture is essential to conserve strength and prevent repetitive stress injuries.

Good posture and body mechanics help to sustain energy.

The most common stances are called the ***horse stance*** and the ***archer stance***.

**Horse Stance** - both feet are placed in line with the edge of the massage table; the knees are kept slightly flexed so that the therapist can apply firmer pressure to the massage movements by shifting the weight from side to side and leaning into the client; the horse stance is the most comfortable stance when doing petrissage on the legs and back.

Back remains erect and relaxed, with the shoulders comfortably dropped and back.

Breathing is deep and full.

**Archer Stance** - position the feet so that an imaginary line drawn through the center of the back foot at the arch passes through the front foot at mid-heel and the third toe; the feet may be close together or a full stride apart; this foot position provides a solid, stable foundation for the therapist to lean into or pull back on a massage movement.

Knees and ankles should be kept slightly flexed; the back remains relatively erect and stable.

Shoulders should remain relaxed and dropped to ensure optimal nerve and blood supply to the hands and arms.

Breathing should be deep and full to supply plenty of oxygen and eliminate carbon dioxide.

***The asymmetric archer's stance is employed for most of the treatment***.

When practicing massage, keep your work directly in front of you and avoid twisting or bending.

Face where you are working, and keep your shoulders, hips, and feet directed toward where your hands are working.

When applying techniques requiring traction, the practitioner grasps the client and leans back, with most of your weight on the front foot.

When a massage calls for deeper pressure, you can apply leverage by leaning into the technique.

**General rule**: it is better to stay behind your work rather than on top of it; maintain an angle of approximately 90 degrees at the shoulder, between the body and the arm.

**General guideline**: is to have a minimum of three feet of clear space on all sides of the table.

Two techniques called ***centering*** and ***grounding*** are important to the practitioner because they provide a psychological, energetic, and physical base from which to work.

**Centering** is based on the concept that you have a geographical center in your body located about two inches below the navel in the pelvic area; known as the ***tan tein*** (***don te-in***) or the ***hara*** in China.

**Centering** is accomplished by focusing awareness on your geographical center (***hara***), breathing fully, and being self-assured.

**Grounding** is based on the concept that you have a connection with the earth and with the client and that you function as a grounding apparatus in helping the client to release tension.

**Grounding** is achieved by mentally visualizing yourself as having the ability to draw from a greater power or energy.

### Protective gear (masks, gloves, gowns, etc)

Health care professionals should assess whether they are at risk of exposure to non intact skin, blood, body fluids, excretions or secretions and choose their items of personal protective equipment according to this risk. Here are some recommendations regarding the use of **PPE (Personal Protective Equipment)**:

The use of PPE does not replace the need for proper hand washing.

PPE is used at all times where contact with blood and body fluids of clients may occur; this includes performing client procedures and clean up procedures.

PPE is only effective in infection control and prevention when applied, used, removed and disposed of properly.

Discard used personal protective equipment in appropriate disposal bags, and dispose of waste appropriately.

A surgical mask helps protect you from inhaling respiratory pathogens transmitted by the droplet route.

Surgical masks provide a barrier that protects the mucous membranes of the mouth and nose which are portals for infection.

Droplets are classified as particles larger than 5μm in size.

***Wear a surgical mask and eye protection or face shield***:

During procedures and client-care activities that are likely to generate splashes or sprays of blood, body fluids, secretions, and excretions.

When you are cleaning contaminated items, linen or handling waste that may generate sprays or splashes of blood, body fluids, secretions, and excretions.

Always wash your hands after you have removed your PPE.

***Gloves may be needed for a variety of reasons***:

When the therapist has a break in the skin or a skin infection on one or both hands

When handling any form of blood, body fluids, secretions, or other unidentifiable substance; this includes the removal of contaminated massage linens and cleaning contaminated equipment

When entering the oral cavity, such as for internal temporomandibular joint massage

When the client requests that the therapist wears gloves

When the therapist does not feel comfortable without them; this requires involving the client and getting an airtight agreement before proceeding with the massage

Gloves may reduce palpatory abilities; gloved hands increase friction.

***Latex glov*es** are very strong, very thin, and conforms to the therapist's hands as though a second skin; a water-based lubricant must be used to prevent material breakdown.

Some people are allergic or sensitive to latex; if symptoms of rashes, itching, or respiratory difficulties occur, remove gloves immediately and seek medical attention.

***Vinyl gloves*** are fine for clients with latex allergies and can be used with oil-based lubricants; they are thicker than latex gloves and greatly reduce tactile sensitivity.

### Self-care

***Use a standard hand washing procedure***.

Wash and dry hands thoroughly before and after performing massage therapy and after using the toilet.

Keep your hands free of blemishes and calluses; use lotion to keep your hands soft and smooth.

Bathe or shower daily and use deodorant as necessary; keep your teeth and gums healthy.

Use mouthwash and avoid foods that contribute to offensive breath odor.

***Wear a clean uniform each day***.

Wear clothing appropriate for your profession.

Do not wear massage uniforms for other purposes.

The uniform should not fit loosely because it will brush up against the client when the therapist leans over the table.

The uniform sleeves should be short to allow for the use of forearms and elbows.

Apply the same protocol for contaminated uniforms as you would in cases of contaminated linens.

Refrain from low-cut necklines and tight or sexually provocative clothing.

***Keep hair clean and away from face.***

Choose a hairstyle that keeps the hair out of the way or secure the hair so that the therapist does not have to move it from his or her face.

Be sure that hair does not touch the client.

Keep facial hair neat and well groomed; if you prefer the clean-shaven look, be sure to shave as often as necessary.

***Avoid wearing ornate jewelry while at work.***

Wearing rings, bracelets, or wristwatches are not advised while performing massage.

Jewelry or any sharp object can potentially injure the client or break the protective barrier of gloves.

***Keep fingernails clean, short, and without nail polish.***

Long fingernails and cracked nail polish provide hiding places for microorganisms.

Long fingernails can injure the client and break the protective barrier of gloves.

Artificial nails present a high risk of fungal infections for the therapist; in rare cases, fungal infections can be transmitted to the client.

Avoid strong fragrances such as perfumes, colognes, and lotions.

Avoid massaging clients who are ill.

Avoid working under the influence of alcohol or recreational drugs.

Avoid gum chewing in the presence of clients.

If you perspire heavily, take precautions to ensure your perspiration does not drop on your client.

### Injury prevention

Massage is a physically demanding profession. Eat a well-balanced, nutritious diet to ensure you have energy to perform and recover from performing massages. It is recommended that a regimen of daily exercise (strength training, stretching) and recovery (regular or self-massage) become a regular part of your lifestyle. Take time for relaxation.

Be aware of good posture and proper body mechanics when walking, standing, sitting, and working.

Poor posture habits such as slouching contribute to fatigue, foot problems, and strain to your back and neck.

## Postural Neck Strain

Looking at our massage strokes requires the head and neck to be in an imbalanced flexed position.

The load on the neck extensors can be eliminated if we do not hold our head and neck in flexion; try not to look at your massage strokes; focus on what you're feeling with your hands.

Keep the head and neck in a neutral, extended position balanced over the trunk while performing the massage.

## Shoulder Strain

When practitioners are manipulating soft tissues, the arms are often held in isometric flexion and/or abduction.

When generating pressure, many massage therapists do so from the shoulders.

Shoulder strain of the deltoid and rotator cuff muscles result from the two above reasons.

Learn to generate pressure from the core of the body.

"When the arms are placed down and in front and against the core of the body as much as possible, the pressure can transfer from the core directly into the forearm, and then the hand into the client (Joseph Muscolino)."

## Carpal Tunnel Syndrome

*Carpal tunnel syndrome* occurs when the median nerve, which runs from the forearm into the palm of the hand, becomes pressed or squeezed at the wrist.

The most problematic posture for carpal tunnel syndrome is full joint extension of the wrist accompanied by finger flexion.

Use of the palm to direct pressure into the client causes carpal tunnel syndrome.

Use the hypothenar eminence or the ulnar side to apply pressure.

Stretching, regular bodywork, self-massage, and conditioning can help prevent carpal tunnel syndrome.

## Tenosynovitis

*Tenosynovitis* is inflammation of the lining of a sheath that surrounds a tendon (the cord that joins muscle to bone).

Commonly experienced by massage therapists at the base of the thumb

*Tenosynovitis* is caused by overuse; excessive use of the tendons of the thumb.

Stretching and self-massage to reduce adhesions to the affected tendons on a regular basis will be helpful.

# Draping

**Draping** is the process of using linens to keep a client covered while receiving a massage.

**Draping** allows the client to be totally undressed and be covered to retain comfort, warmth, and modesty.

It gives the practitioner the freedom to massage all parts of the body unencumbered by the client's clothing.

Proper draping ensures that the client stays warm and feels safe and comfortable.

## Safe and appropriate

Uncover only the portion of the body that is being massaged.

Ensure that the genitals, gluteal cleft, and breasts (private areas) are always draped.

## Communication

Massage stimulates the parasympathetic nervous system, affecting the basal body temperature, which may result in the client becoming cold.

Ask your client if they are comfortably warm in the beginning and at the middle of the massage session.

If your client indicates they are cold, place a flannel blanket over the top drape or have a massage table heating pad on the table (under the fitted sheet) prior to beginning the session.

If your client becomes too warm, uncover the arms and legs.

If you accidentally expose our client, acknowledge your error by pardoning yourself, while looking away to redrape the exposed area.

When the client is turning from supine to prone, instruct the client to, "Please roll over by turning toward me and then roll over onto your stomach."

If a face cradle is used, instruct the client to, "Slide up the table until your face is comfortably situated on the cradle."

When a client is turning from prone to supine, instruct the client to: "Please roll over by turning away from me and then roll over onto your back."

If your client is prone and using the face rest, instruct the client to, "Scoot down until your head is resting on the table and off the face cradle."

## Draping Methods

### Top Cover Method

Uses a table covering (fitted sheet) along with a top covering large enough to cover the entire body.

***Towel Draping*** - Use two bath-sized towels as a top cover.

The two towels are in a T configuration; the upper towel lying across the torso (horizontally) and the lower towel covering the lower extremities up to the hips.

The lower towel is turned crossways (horizontally) over the central area of the body (the hips) when it is time for the client to turn over.

***Sheet Draping*** - for the top covering, a twin-size sheet is preferred or one half of a full or double sheet; minimum size for the top cover is 72 inches long and 36 inches wide.

The top covering (sheet) is arranged on the bottom sheet with the top edge folded down to reveal the bottom sheet.

When massaging specific areas of the body, the top covering (sheet) may be tucked under the client's body; untuck the sheet and redrape the area before moving to another area to massage.

The top cover sheet can serve as the wrap the client uses to get from the dressing area to the table and from the table to the dressing area.

# Business Practices

## Business Planning

Business planning starts when a business is first conceived and continues throughout the life of the business.

**Planning** involves clarifying your purpose, stating your mission, setting goals, and determining priorities.

Purpose is a theme that is derived from your dreams and ideals; (ex. to make a positive difference for my clientele).

**Mission Statement** is a short general statement of the main focus of the business; it expresses the values and intent of the business; used on promotional material as a reflection of the business's public image.

**Goals** are specific, attainable, measurable things or accomplishments that you decide on and make a commitment to achieve.

Setting goals clarifies your intentions and directs your creative energy toward realizing your dreams; goals can be short or long term; ex. I will see 20 clients per week.

Keep your goals personalized and in the present tense.

## Strategic Planning

**Strategic planning** is about breaking down a difficult problem into manageable chunks.

Start with your major goal, analyze it, and break it down into smaller goals and steps.

Make a master list of the activities required to achieve the major goal and use separate sheets for each project.

Transfer your goals and items from strategic planning sheets to a calendar or a simple document on your computer.

### Action Steps for Strategic Planning

List current date and target date for accomplishing goal

Identify the major goal; describe the existing situation; list the benefits of achieving the goal

Brainstorm possible courses of action; choose the best solution; outline an action plan

Determine possible challenges and solutions; identify required resources; outline action steps and target date for each step

## Strategic Planning benefits

You are less likely to forget a major step; creative ideas and brainstorming come easier

Goals become clarified and more real; you realize that some steps may require more immediate action than others

A more accurate timetable is developed; a written description of your intentions is a self-motivation tool

### Office Management

Establish a space that's dedicated exclusively to your business that includes a writing surface (preferably a desk), an ergonomic chair, a desk lamp, a filing cabinet/drawer, and office supplies.

Minimize handling of paper by dividing all paperwork into four initial categories: take action, file, trash, and read/review later.

Set a specific time of day to open mail/email; the goal is to handle mail once.

Whenever possible, take immediate action such as write a return letter/email, file the information, or trash it.

Return calls within 24 hours and store paper, pen, appointment book, and new client checklist within reach.

Keep track of contacts and potential business resources using your computer contact manager or place sheets in a binder with alphabetical dividers.

Include the person's name, company, title, work address and phone number, home address and phone number, email address, who referred you, where you met, and action to be taken

List the dates and times of any actions directly onto the contact form

Keep client files in alphabetical order; design a one-page checklist and staple it to the left side of the folder; put the client contact information on top of the form and include other pertinent details.

Review all client files at least twice a year; in general, keep all records at least 10 years (indefinitely is ideal).

Develop a tickler file for upcoming events; a tickler file reminds you of your commitments and assists in follow-through; it contains 12 separate sections (one for each month) and a set of dividers numbered 1-31, for each day of the month.

Check your tickler file daily; look at the current day and possibly the next two days

The rule of thumb for financial record keeping is: Keep all receipts.

The two major ways for keeping financial receipts are: by the category (ex. Marketing Expenses, Supplies), or by the date (one file folder for each month of the year).

## Marketing

**Marketing** is simply sharing information about yourself and your services with potential and current clients so they get a sense of who you are. **Marketing** allows the client to make an informed choice of whether to use your services.

**Marketing** is the business activity done to promote and increase business. **Word of mouth** is the best advertising.

The major portion of marketing a service business is educational in nature; actively educate the public about what you do and how it can benefit them.

The goal of marketing is to create and maintain a thriving practice.

Establishing Credibility is the foundation of any successful marketing venture and is essential to the long-term success of your practice.

Establish your credibility, promote and build up contacts by providing or volunteering your services at health expos and fairs, community events, conventions, store openings, sporting events and at organizations that your target market attends.

Establish your credibility and increase your visibility by arranging speaking engagements, presenting workshops and demonstrations.

Concentrate on client referrals, direct mail, and targeted advertising to announce special services.

Target markets/groups are various segments of the population that have similar characteristics.

Target groups can be broad: women, athletes, elderly people, or professional persons; Target groups can be specific: pregnant women, teachers, low-birth weight infants, or female runners.

Two ways to determine your target market: First, consider which type of clientele that you want to attract, and then contact clubs and organizations that cater to persons from that group.

Create brochures highlighting the benefits of massage for the specific conditions common to that group; Make personal contact with people and participate in activities common to your target market.

The **Brochure** is the primary tool for educating the public and potential clients about the services offered.

It should give specifics about the nature of the services offered, a description of the services offered, the qualifications of the practitioner, the client's financial and time investment, the client's role in health care.

Secondly, assess your client files to determine who is presently using your services and what they have in common; Design promotional activities that reach that segment of the population.

When starting out, talk with everyone about your profession: family, friends, neighbors, and people in line at the grocery store, movies, and DMV.

Give free sessions in the beginning to establish credibility and build relationships; it is best if those free sessions are given to people who are likely to become clients or actively generate word-of-mouth referrals.

Wear logo clothing with your profession or slogan emblazoned on it. Always carry your business cards.

Post your business cards and brochures wherever your target markets are likely to see them. Build a professional website to describe your services, book appointments, provide educational information, list policies and procedures, and prices for services.

The Massage Chair is an excellent promotional tool to familiarize the public with the experience of touch and the benefits of massage.

Advertising includes magazine and newspaper ads and listings, signs, embossed pens and calendars, and similar materials.

Networking is developing personal and professional contacts for the purpose of giving and receiving support and sharing resources and information.

Encourage Referrals: word-of-mouth advertising is the best advertising that there is; to promote referrals from other professionals, give them a treatment so that they can experience firsthand what you have to offer.

Remember the three **R's** of referrals: **Request** referrals from satisfied clients; **Reward** those who send you referrals with prompt thank-you cards or personal telephone calls; **Reciprocate** by sending referrals or using the services of those who send you referrals.

## Hiring/Interviewing

Expanding your practice by hiring other therapists or support staff can increase your potential to provide services to more people.

Hiring office support staff for administrative tasks, such as scheduling, confirming appointments, purchasing supplies, and organizing client records can free you up to spend more time with clients or focus on marketing tasks to grow your business.

Hiring employees increases the employer's responsibility for record keeping and tax regulations.

The most common manner in which practitioners enlist/hire additional help is by including other massage therapists in their business, usually as contract labor.

When doing so, the massage therapist is an independent contractor and is hired as his/her own boss for a per-client fee or a percentage without taxes, workers' compensation, or Social Security/Medicare being deducted from wages.

An **independent contractor** is self-employed and is responsible for his/her own taxes; if you pay an independent contractor **$600 or more** in the course of a year, you are required to file IRS tax forms **1099** and **1096**.

Sign "**independent contractor**" contracts which clearly state the requirements of all parties while making it clear the contractors are free to pursue other clients.

Independent contractors must provide their own tables, linens, products, music and other supplies and provide their own insurance and workers' compensation coverage.

**Independent contractor liability insurance** protects the contractor against third-party claims from hired independent contractors.

Allow contractors to set their own schedules (**no more than 10 hours per week** or on an as-needed basis for special events); request copies of contractors' tax returns.

Get legal counsel to develop an independent contractor agreement; include a work description for each subcontracting assignment along with a policy and procedure statement.

Anyone who performs services subject to the will and control of an employer, as to both what must be done and how it must be done is an employee.

Two primary characteristics of an employer-employee relationship are: an employer has a right to discharge an employee and an employer supplies the employee with tools and a place to work.

If the business owner has a right to control how and when a person works, then that person is most likely an employee.

As an employer, you must match employee **FICA** (Social Security and Medicare) deductions; pay **FUTA** (Federal Unemployment Tax Act), pay state unemployment taxes; provide workers' compensation; withhold state and federal taxes; deposit withheld taxes; prepare quarterly payroll tax returns; and send W-2 forms to employees annually.

**Form SS-4** (Application for Employer Identification Number) and **Form W-4** (Employee's Withholding Allowance Certificate) are needed by you the employer.

The employer needs a Federal Employer's Identification Number (**EIN**) and a state EIN.

All employees must fill out **Form I-9** (Employment Eligibility Verification) from the U.S. Department of Justice, Immigration and Naturalization Service.

Administrative support staff is often the first point of contact that a potential client has with your business; your support staff establishes the persona of your business, its image and philosophy.

Identify what type of support you need; determine whether the position is part or full time, the hours you require and the wage rate according to the demands of the position and the skill level.

Establish the position's duties, responsibilities and the personality you need to project the persona of your business.

Design your interview questions to elicit the most information about your candidates and whether they fit into the mold you have established for the job.

### Documentation and Records

**Documentation** provides historical perspective, protects you in case of legal actions, demonstrates professionalism, and verifies progress.

Insurance companies will not honor your malpractice coverage if you fail to keep accurate and detailed records.

It is recommended that you have a sign-in sheet; the sign-in sheet is your protection, it verifies the client was there.

## Client records

### *Client files serve three major purposes*:

1. Record keeping (client's name, address, phone number, session dates and amounts paid)

2. Up-to-date files document a client's needs and progress, which help to develop the most effective treatment.

3. Client files provide documentation necessary for insurance reimbursement.

Facts to include on your client intake form are: client's name, address, phone numbers, medical history, chief complaint, current medication, and reason(s) for using your services.

Updated client files help the practitioner to render prompt and efficient service, ensure access to current information about the client, and provide some legal protection for the practitioner in cases of litigation.

Record keeping for clients involves the written record of intake procedures, including informed consent, needs assessments (including history and physical assessment), obtaining release of information, and the ongoing process of recording each session (**charting**).

**Charting** is the process of keeping a written record that emphasizes a problem-solving approach to client care; it is the ongoing record of each client session (**SOAP Notes**)

**SOAP Notes:** *Subjective* - a description of symptoms and conditions as described by the client or the referring primary healthcare provider; these notes reflect a client's perception of his conditions.

*Objective* - an account of your observations and results of the treatments you administer.

*Assessment* - a record of the changes in a client's condition as a result of treatment.

*Plan* - a list of recommended action and client preferences.

A treatment plan provides a kind of blueprint for the sessions that is updated periodically.

The appointment book is possibly the most important document for organizing a successful and prosperous business, and it is an important time management tool.

Make sure that any abbreviations used are universally understood, or write out the word; Use black pen or type the notes; never erase or white-out a correction, draw a single line through the error, and make the correction above or next to the error.

## Business records

**Business records** are necessary to meet the requirements of local, state, and federal laws pertaining to taxes and employees.

Open a separate account under the name of the business, and deposit all business income into the account; this will provide a record of your earnings.

Pay all business bills by check, or a debit/credit card that provides a record of your expenditures.

Be sure to record clearly in the check register the check number, the date that the check was written, to whom the check was written, what the check was written for, and the amount of the check.

Two basic steps to recording business income: 1. when the income is first received and an invoice or sales slip is filled out; 2. when the invoices are totaled, summarized, and recorded in an income ledger.

Invoices should be written in duplicate; the original goes to the client and the copy goes into the cash box or daily records; the invoices are tallied and recorded on the income ledger.

The **disbursement ledger** is your record of all of the expenditures that the business pays out, including bills, loan payments, payroll, and the money that you pay yourself.

The function of the disbursement ledger is to separate and classify business expenditures for tax purposes and to identify where your money is going.

Obtain and keep receipts for all expenditures and record them in the disbursement ledger.

Keep all receipts, ledgers, and canceled checks a minimum of seven years in case of an audit.

Keep tax returns, real estate, and business contracts indefinitely.

A **Profit and Loss Statement (P&L)** is a summary of the income (revenue) and disbursement registers for a particular period (monthly, quarterly, and annually).

To prepare a P&L statement, list all sources of income and the amount collected from each source; add the amounts to determine the total revenues.

Next, list all expense categories and the amount spent for each category; add those amounts to determine the total expense.

Subtract the total expense from the total revenue to determine the net profit or loss for the particular period.

**Accounts receivable** is a record of money's owed to you by other persons or businesses; require cash payments at the time of service for everything except gift certificates, advance payments, insurance billings, and credit card payments.

**Accounts payable** records the money that you owe to other persons or businesses; file statements and purchase orders so that you have an accurate record when it is time to pay the bills.

All business related travel should be recorded for tax purposes; expenses for operating a vehicle for business are deductible from taxable income.

The mileage to and from your home or office to do an outcall is deductible; keep a mileage log and record all business travel.

For each trip, record the destination, beginning and ending odometer readings, total miles traveled, and purpose of the trip.

If you deduct the actual auto expense, keep an itemized record of all expenses (fuel, service, license fees, parking, and depreciation records of actual purchase); the auto expense is prorated between business use and personal use.

## Healthcare and Business Terminology

In healthcare/medical terminology, long words are compound words constructed of prefixes, root words, and suffixes. A **prefix** is one or more syllables added in front of the root word to further its meaning.

**Prefixes**: a- absent, without, away from; ab- away from; ad- to, toward; an- without;

anti- against; ante- before; auto- self; bi- two; bio- life; carcin-(o) cancer; circum- around

co- with, together; contra- against, opposite; de- down, from; dia- across, through, apart

di- two; dis- apart, away from; dors- back; dys- abnormal, impaired; e- out, from

ecto- outside, without; end-(o) inside, within; epi- over, upon; eryth- red; ex- out of;

extra- beyond, outside of; flex- bent; front- front, forehead; hemi- half; hetero- the other

hom- common, same; hydro- denoting water; hyper- above, extreme; hypo- under, below

in- within, into, not; infra- beneath; inter- between; intra- inside, within; leuk-(o) white

macro- large; mal- abnormal, bad; medi- midline, middle; mega- large, extreme; micro- small; mono- one, single; multi- many, multiple; narc- stupor, numbness; neo- new necro- dead; nutri- nourish; para- next to, resembling, beside; path- pertaining to disease; per- through; peri- around; poly- many, much; post- after, later in time

pre-, pro- before in time; pseudo- false; quad- four; re- back, again; retro- backward; semi- half; sub- under, below; super- above, in addition; supra- over, above, upper; syn- together

tri- three; trans- across; uni- single, one

The **root word** generally indicates the body part or structure involved; occasionally, two or more root words are combined to show relation or position (e.g., cardiopulmonary/heart and lung). Many root words add an "o" or an "i at the end when combined with other words.

abdomin abdomen; adren adrenal; arteri artery; aur ear; arth(o) joint; brachi arm; bronch bronchial; cardi heart; cephal head; cerebro brain; cervic neck; chondr(o) cartilage; cost rib

crani skull; cyst bladder, cyst; cyt cell; dent teeth; derm skin; encephal brain; entero intestine; fibr fiber; gastr(o) stomach; gyn woman; hem blood; hepat liver; hist tissue

hydr water; labi lip; mamm breast; my(o) muscle; nephr(o) kidney; neur(o) nerve; ocul eye; oss ost(e) bone; ot ear; ped child, foot; phleb vein; pneum lung; pod foot; psych mind

pulmo lung; rhin nose; therm heat; thorac chest; throm clot; thyr thyroid; toxic poison; ur urine; uter uterus; vas vessel; ven vein; vertebr spine

A **suffix** is added to the end of the word; **suffixes** often denote a diagnosis, symptom, or surgical procedure or identify a word as a known or adjective.

-al, -ar pertaining to an area; -algia painful condition; -ase denoting an enzyme; -cyte cell;

-desis a binding; -ectomy surgical removal of a body part; -emia blood condition

-genic producing or causing; -gram a record; -graph write, draw, record; -ia a noun ending of a condition; -ic a noun/adjective ending; -ism condition; -ist one who does

-itis inflammation; -meter a devise for measuring; -oid resembling; -ology study of, science of; -oma tumor; -osis abnormal condition; -ostomy forming an opening

-otomy incision, cutting into; -pathic diseased; -plegia paralysis; -phobia morbid fear of

-rrhea profuse flow; -scope examination instrument; -scopy a procedure using a scope

-tomy surgical procedure

## Business Terminology

**Business plan**: a written document that describes in detail how a new business is going to achieve its goals; it should include a business model (how you will make money), a competitive analysis and marketing strategy, how you will operate and financial projections.

**Business name**: select a business name; make sure it is legally available and trademark it; if you will be using a DBA/Fictitious name statement (doing business as), file a DBA with your city/county.

**Legal form of business**: *Sole proprietorship* - is an individual business owner responsible for all expenses, obligations, liabilities, and assets.

*Partnership* - is a business model in which two or more partners share responsibility and benefits of running a business.

*Corporation* - is a business setup subject to state regulation and taxation; a charter must be obtained from the state in which the corporation operates.

*Limited liability companies* (*LLC*) - are a form of legal entity, something between a partnership and a corporation; the owners of an *LLC* are a separate entity from the business and are shielded from some of the personal liability of the business.

**Required business licenses and permits**: Planning and zoning permits - required to ensure that the operation and location of the business complies with local zoning requirements.

**Building safety permit** - might be issued after the place of business has been inspected and found to be free of conditions that could pose a hazard to you or your clients and comply with building and fire codes.

**Business license** - might be required to operate a business in the city, county, or state.

**Massage license** - can be a city, county, or state requirement to perform massage services for a fee.

**Employer's identification number (EIN)** - the federal tax identification number issued to businesses and is used on all tax-related forms; an EIN is required of partnerships and businesses that hire employees; Sole proprietors can use an EIN or Social Security number.

**Sales tax permit** - required if you sell products or if services are taxed.

**Provider's number** - an identification number issued to licensed health care providers; used and required when submitting claims to and receiving payment from medical insurance companies for services rendered.

Massage practitioners are not eligible to hold a provider's number, but do receive third-party payments (insurance payments) by contracting with, billing through, or being an employee of a licensed provider (e.g., doctor, chiropractor, physical therapist).

**Business location**: depending on your industry, you may choose to run your business from home (check with the city's zoning regulations to see if it's legal); usually the zoning that a massage business requires is general office or commercial zoning.

**Business insurance**: adequate insurance against fire, theft, and liability is necessary to protect the business.

**Liability insurance** - covers costs of injuries and litigation resulting from injuries sustained on your property; usually a part of a homeowner's policy but might not cover business-related occurrences.

**Professional liability insurance** - also called malpractice insurance, protects the therapist from lawsuits filed by a client because of injury or loss resulting from alleged negligence or substandard performance of a professional skill.

**Automobile insurance** - full coverage provides medical and liability insurance to the driver and any passengers, and covers the vehicle and its contents regardless of who is at fault.

**Property insurance** or **fire and theft insurance** - covers fixtures, furniture, equipment, products, and supplies.

**Renter's insurance** - covers the loss of furniture and equipment in the case of theft, vandalism, fire, or other natural disasters.

**Medical/health insurance** - helps cover the cost of medical bills, especially hospitalization, serious injury, or illness.

**Disability insurance** - protects the person from loss of income when he/she is unable to work because of long-term illness or injury.

**Worker's compensation insurance** - is required if you have employees; it covers the medical costs for employees if they are injured on the job.

**Business bank account**: a business bank account is needed to receive and make payments, pay taxes, and pays employees; keep your business and personal accounts separate.

**Business website/email**: purchase a domain (URL/website address) for your business and get business email under that domain so your business looks professional.

**Marketing materials**: include a business website and business cards; you may also want to develop brochures, fliers, price sheets, and other printed materials.

**Recourse policy**: the purpose of the recourse policy is to act as a guide for addressing client issues; it could be a refund or offering of complimentary massage in the event of an unsatisfactory experience.

# Bibliography

Beck, Mark F. *Theory & Practice of Therapeutic Massage.* 5th ed. Clifton Park: Milady, 2011. Print

Biel, Andrew. *Trail Guide to the Body.* 4th ed. Boulder: Books of Discovery, 2010. Print

Fritz, Sandy. *Mosby's Essential Sciences for Therapeutic Massage: Anatomy, Physiology, Biomechanics, and Pathology.* 2nd ed. St. Louis: Mosby, 2004. Print

Fritz, Sandy. *Mosby's Fundamentals of Therapeutic Massage.* 2nd ed. St. Louis: Mosby, 2000. Print

Kendall, Florence, et al. *Muscle Testing and Function with Posture and Pain.* 5th ed. Baltimore: Lippincott Williams & Wilkins, 2005. Print

Martini, Frederic H., Michael J. Timmons, and Robert B. Tallitsch. *Human Anatomy.* 6th ed. San Francisco: Pearson Benjamin Cummings, 2009. Print

Sohnen-Moe, Cherie. *Business Mastery.* 4th ed. Tucson: Sohnen-Moe Associates Inc., 2008. Print

Werner, Ruth. *A Massage Therapist's Guide to Pathology.* 5th ed. China: Lippincott Williams & Wilkins, 2013. Print

"Self-Care: Common Injuries and How to Prevent Them." *American Massage Therapy Association.* AMTA.org, 29 Apr. 2014. Web. 15 June 2015

"Standards of Practice." *College of Massage Therapists of Ontario.* CMTO.com, n.d. Web. 21 July 2015

## About the Author

Charles Everett is a certified massage therapist and personal trainer. He is an avid fitness enthusiast and former Air Force super heavyweight boxing champion. He currently resides in California.